MATH Trailblazers®

A BALANCED MATHEMATICS PROGRAM INTEGRATING SCIENCE AND LANGUAGE ARTS

Unit Resource Guide
Unit 13

Ratio and Proportion

THIRD EDITION

KENDALL/HUNT PUBLISHING COMPANY
4050 Westmark Drive   Dubuque, Iowa 52002

A TIMS® Curriculum
University of Illinois at Chicago

UIC The University of Illinois at Chicago

The original edition was based on work supported by the National Science Foundation under grant No. MDR 9050226 and the University of Illinois at Chicago. Any opinions, findings, and conclusions or recommendations expressed in this publication are those of the author(s) and do not necessarily reflect the views of the granting agencies.

Letter Home

Ratio and Proportion

Date: _____

Dear Family Member:

In this unit, students focus on the concepts of ratio and proportion. Ratios and proportions are used in everyday life and in the specialized worlds of math, science, art, music, and architecture. Speed, a comparison of distance per time, is a commonly used ratio. Number of miles traveled per gallon of gas is another common ratio. Ratios are found at the grocery store where the price for apples may be 3 pounds for 89¢. Proportional thinking is used when doubling or tripling a recipe or when figuring out prices in a foreign currency. In mathematics, understanding proportions is necessary for understanding concepts in algebra and geometry.

The unit begins with ratios in students' own lives and proceeds to an examination of the use of proportional reasoning in science. Students explore why some objects sink in water and others float.

Students find the ratio of an object's mass to its volume to help understand why objects sink or float.

You can help your child at home by:

- Pointing out comparisons made with ratios whenever they occur. Some places to look are the miles per gallon ratings for cars, the exchange rates for currencies, and the prices for groceries.
- Asking your child to help you adjust a recipe to serve more people when you are cooking.

Sincerely,

_____

Carta al hogar

Razón y proporción

Fecha: _____

Estimado miembro de familia:

En esta unidad, los estudiantes estudiarán los conceptos de razones y proporciones. Las razones y las proporciones se usan en la vida cotidiana y en los ámbitos especializados de las matemáticas, la ciencia, el arte, la música y la arquitectura. Una razón común es la velocidad, que es una comparación de la distancia recorrida en cierto tiempo. Otra razón común es el número de millas recorrido por galón de gasolina. Las razones también se usan en las tiendas, por ejemplo cuando el precio de las manzanas es 3 libras por 89¢. Las proporciones se usan cuando se duplican o triplican los ingredientes de una receta o cuando se calculan precios en moneda extranjera. En las matemáticas, entender las proporciones es un requisito para entender conceptos de álgebra y geometría.

La unidad comienza con razones que los estudiantes usan en sus propias vidas y continúa con una explicación del uso del razonamiento proporcional en la ciencia. Los estudiantes investigan por qué algunos objetos se hunden y otros flotan.

Los estudiantes hallan la razón de la masa de un objeto a su volumen para entender por qué los objetos se hunden o flotan.

Usted puede ayudar a su hijo/a en casa:

- Señalando comparaciones hechas con razones cada vez que ocurren. Algunos ejemplos son las calificaciones de los automóviles según las millas que recorren por galón de gasolina, el tipo de cambio de monedas y los precios de alimentos.
- Pidiéndole a su hijo/a que le ayude modificar una receta para servir a más gente cuando cocine.

Atentamente,

_____

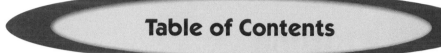

Unit 13
Ratio and Proportion

Unit 13

Outline
Ratio and Proportion

Unit Summary

Estimated Class Sessions
10-15

This unit's goal is to use ratio and proportion to develop formal concepts and procedures for solving problems that involve proportional reasoning. Students review the use of words, tables, graphs, and symbols to express ratios. They learn that a proportion is a statement that two ratios are equivalent and develop strategies for solving proportional reasoning problems. Students apply proportional reasoning to the study of density in the activity *Sink and Float* and the lab *Mass vs. Volume*.

Major Concept Focus

- ratios
- variables in proportion
- volume
- TIMS Laboratory Method
- using ratios and proportions to solve problems
- proportions
- mass
- density
- point graphs
- best-fit lines

Pacing Suggestions

This unit is designed to be completed in 10 to 15 days.

- Lesson 2 *Variables in Proportion* is an optional lesson that extends students' knowledge of algebraic concepts including using variables and proportional reasoning.
- Lesson 3 *Sink and Float* and Lesson 4 *Mass vs. Volume: Proportions and Density* make strong connections between mathematics and science. Students can collect the data for these investigations during science time.
- Lesson 5 *Problems of Scale* includes a series of word problems and a quiz. You can assign the problems for homework to prepare students for the quiz. They are also appropriate for use by a substitute teacher since preparation is minimal.

Assessment Indicators

Use the following Assessment Indicators and the *Observational Assessment Record* that follows the Background section in this unit to assess students on key ideas.

A1. Can students use words, tables, graphs, fractions, and colon notation to express ratios?

A2. Can students use ratios and proportions to solve problems?

A3. Can students measure mass?

A4. Can students measure volume by displacement?

A5. Can students collect, organize, graph, and analyze data?

A6. Can students draw and interpret best-fit lines?

A7. Do students solve problems in more than one way?

A8. Can students choose appropriate methods and tools to calculate (calculators, pencil and paper, or mental math)?

Unit Planner

	Lesson Information	Supplies	Copies/Transparencies
Lesson 1 **Ratios, Recipes, and Proportions** URG Pages 24–38 SG Pages 396–401 DPP A–D HP Parts 1–2 & 5 *Estimated Class Sessions* **2–3**	**Activity** Students explore ratios and proportions in recipes. **Math Facts** DPP Bit A reviews division facts for the square numbers. **Homework** 1. Assign the Homework section in the *Student Guide.* 2. Assign Parts 1–2 of the Home Practice. **Assessment** 1. Use *Questions 21–23* of the Peanut Cake section in the *Student Guide* to assess students' abilities to write ratios and use proportions. 2. Assign Part 5 of the Home Practice to assess students' fluency in solving problems involving ratio and proportion. 3. Use the *Observational Assessment Record* to note students' abilities to express ratios using words, tables, graphs, fractions, and colon notations.	• 1 calculator per student	• 1 copy of *Centimeter Graph Paper* URG Page 34 per student • 1 copy of *Observational Assessment Record* URG Pages 11–12 to be used throughout this unit • 1 transparency of *Centimeter Graph Paper* URG Page 34
Lesson 2 **Variables in Proportion** URG Pages 39–53 SG Pages 402–410 *Estimated Class Sessions* **2–3**	OPTIONAL LESSON **Optional Activity** Students review selected topics in the fifth-grade curriculum and explore them from the perspective of ratio and proportion. They extend their knowledge of algebraic concepts as they investigate properties of variables in proportion and explore the use of line graphs in solving proportions. **Homework** 1. Assign the Homework section in the *Student Guide.* 2. Assign problems from Lesson 5.	• 1 calculator per student • large graph paper, optional	• 2 copies of *Centimeter Graph Paper* URG Page 34 per student • 4 transparencies of *Centimeter Graph Paper* URG Page 34, optional
Lesson 3 **Sink and Float** URG Pages 54–73 SG Pages 411–414 DAB Page 205 DPP E–J HP Part 3 *Estimated Class Sessions* **3**	**Activity** Students measure the mass and volume of several objects. Then they find the ratio of the mass to the volume (density) of each object and use it to predict whether the object will sink or float in water. **Math Facts** Use DPP items E, H, and I to review division facts. **Homework** Assign Part 3 of the Home Practice. **Assessment** Use the *Observational Assessment Record* to note students' abilities to use ratios and proportions to solve problems.	• 1 two-pan balance per student group • 1 set of gram masses per student group • 1 250-cc graduated cylinder per student group • 1 100-cc graduated cylinder per student group • 1 small piece of clay for leveling the balance per student group • paper towels • water	• 1 copy of *Mass Review* URG Pages 64–65 per student, optional • 1 copy of *Volume Review* URG Pages 66–68 per student, optional

	Lesson Information	**Supplies**	**Copies/ Transparencies**
		• 1 eyedropper per student group	
		• 1 cup or beaker for pouring water per student group	
		• 1 large container (dishpan) of water per student group	
		• several small objects that sink or float (rock, marble, cork, clay, 1-inch diameter steel or plastic sphere, wood, paraffin block) per student group	
		• 1 ruler to measure paraffin per student group	
		• 1 calculator per student group	

Lesson 4

Mass vs. Volume: Proportions and Density

URG Pages 74–97
SG Pages 415–422

DPP K–R
HP Part 4

Estimated Class Sessions
4-5

Lab
Students use ratios and graphs to explore whether the density of a material is constant or dependent upon the amount of the material. They use proportional reasoning to solve problems about mass, volume, and density. Then they explore patterns in graphs that help them predict whether objects will sink or float.

Math Facts
DPP items M and Q review division facts.

Homework
Assign homework *Questions 1–7* in the *Student Guide*.

Assessment
1. Assign Home Practice Part 4.
2. Grade the lab by assigning points to each part.
3. Use the *Observational Assessment Record* to assess students' abilities to measure mass and volume.
4. Transfer appropriate documentation from the Unit 13 *Observational Assessment Record* to students' *Individual Assessment Record Sheets*.

Supplies:
• 5 ½-inch-diameter steel spheres per student group
• 1 1-inch-diameter steel sphere per student group
• 1 1¼-inch-diameter steel sphere per student group
• enough clay to make 3 pieces about the same size as the steel spheres and a small piece for leveling the balance; (clay cannot be water soluble) per student group
• 1 two-pan balance per student group
• 1 set of gram masses per student group
• 1 250-cc graduated cylinder per student group
• 1 100-cc graduated cylinder per student group

Copies/Transparencies:
• 2 copies of *Centimeter Graph Paper* URG Page 34 per student
• 2 copies of *Three-column Data Table* URG Page 91 per student
• 2 transparencies of *Centimeter Graph Paper* URG Page 34
• 1 copy of *Individual Assessment Record Sheet* TIG Assessment section per student, previously copied for use throughout the year

(Continued)

	Lesson Information	Supplies	Copies/Transparencies
		• paper towels • 1 eyedropper per student group • water • 1 cup or beaker for pouring water per student group • 1 calculator per student group • vegetable oil, corn syrup, clear soda, raisins, eggs, salt, and food coloring for the extension	
Lesson 5 **Problems of Scale** URG Pages 98–105 SG Page 423 DPP S–T *Estimated Class Sessions* **1**	**Activity** Students solve word problems and take a quiz on content from this unit. **Math Facts** DPP item S provides practice with the division facts. **Homework** Assign some or all of the questions for homework. **Assessment** Use the *Paint Quiz* as an assessment.	• 1 calculator per student • 1 ruler per student	• 1 copy of *Paint Quiz* URG Pages 102–103 per student

Preparing for Upcoming Lessons

In Unit 14 Lessons 1 and 2, students measure the circumference and diameter of cans and lids. Ask students to bring in cans and lids of various sizes. A good selection for students to measure includes empty spools of thread, film canisters, soup cans, masking tape rolls, coffee cans, and large lids.

Connections

A current list of literature and software connections is available at *www.mathtrailblazers.com*. You can also find information on connections in the *Teacher Implementation Guide* Literature List and Software List sections.

Literature Connections
Suggested Titles
- Carter, Andy, and Carol Saller. *George Washington Carver.* Carolrhoda Books, Inc. Minneapolis, MN, 2001. (Lesson 1)

Software Connections
- *Graph Master* allows students to collect data and create their own graphs.
- *Math Munchers Deluxe* provides practice in basic facts and finding equivalent fractions, decimals, percents, ratios, angles and identifying geometric shapes, factors, and multiples in an arcade-like game.
- *Math Mysteries: Measurement* develops multistep problem solving with distance, weight, and capacity.
- *TinkerPlots* allows students to record, compare, and analyze data in tables and graphs.

Teaching All Math Trailblazers Students

Math Trailblazers® lessons are designed for students with a wide range of abilities. The lessons are flexible and do not require significant adaptation for diverse learning styles or academic levels. However, when needed, lessons can be tailored to allow students to engage their abilities to the greatest extent possible while building knowledge and skills.

To assist you in meeting the needs of all students in your classroom, this section contains information about some of the features in the curriculum that allow all students access to mathematics. For additional information, see the Teaching the *Math Trailblazers* Student: Meeting Individual Needs section in the *Teacher Implementation Guide.*

Differentiation Opportunities in this Unit

Laboratory Experiments

Laboratory experiments enable students to solve problems using a variety of representations including pictures, tables, graphs, and symbols. Teachers can assign or adapt parts of the analysis according to the student's ability. The following lesson is a lab:

- Lesson 4 *Mass vs. Volume: Proportions and Density*

DPP Challenges

DPP Challenges are items from the Daily Practice and Problems that usually take more than fifteen minutes to complete. These problems are more thought-provoking and can be used to stretch students' problem-solving skills. The following lessons have DPP Challenges in them:

- DPP Challenge D from Lesson 1 *Ratios, Recipes, and Proportions*
- DPP Challenges P and R from Lesson 4 *Mass vs. Volume: Proportions and Density*
- DPP Challenge T from Lesson 5 *Problems of Scale*

Extensions

Use extensions to enrich lessons. Many extensions provide opportunities to further involve or challenge students of all abilities. Take a moment to review the extensions prior to beginning this unit. Some extensions may require additional preparation and planning. The following lessons contain extensions:

- Lesson 3 *Sink and Float*
- Lesson 4 *Mass vs. Volume: Proportions and Density*

Background
Ratio and Proportion

A major theme throughout the *Math Trailblazers* curriculum is the development of proportional reasoning. This unit's goal is to bring together previously studied concepts of ratio and proportion with more formal ideas and strategies. Students are developing many tools and strategies for solving problems requiring proportional reasoning. For example, in fifth grade in the lab *Distance vs. Time* in Unit 3, students solved problems using data they collected on the walking speed of fifth graders. They organized their data in a table and graphed the data using a point graph. Sample data and a graph for the lab are shown in Figure 1.

With the table and graph students can use many strategies to solve problems such as, *"How long will it take the student to travel 18 yards?"* They can use patterns in the data table, use extrapolation on the graph, find equal ratios, or use multiplication. Students work within the context of the lab to solve more difficult problems such as, *"How far can a fifth grader walk in one minute? How far can a fifth grader walk in one hour?"*

In this unit, students use these strategies and concepts as a foundation while developing more formal concepts and procedures to solve problems involving proportional reasoning. They learn that a **proportion** is a statement that two ratios are equivalent.

Distance vs. Time

Time in Seconds	Distance in Yards	$\dfrac{D}{t}$ Ratio in $\dfrac{yd}{sec}$
2	3	$\dfrac{3}{2}$
4	6	$\dfrac{6}{4}$
6	9	$\dfrac{9}{6}$

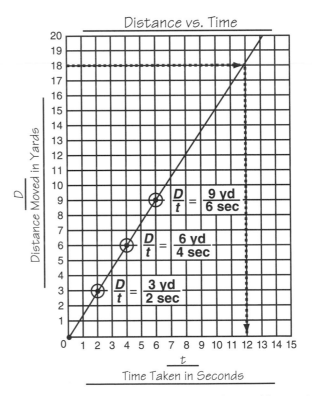

Figure 1: *In Unit 3 students used data tables and graphs to solve proportional reasoning problems about speed.*

In an optional lesson, students can review data tables and graphs from experiments and activities in previous units to formalize and extend algebraic concepts of variables in proportion. They look for similarities in the data tables and graphs and make generalizations about some of the important properties of **variables in proportion.** Two variables in an experiment are in proportion if their ratio is always the same. For example, we know that the two variables in the experiment *Distance vs. Time* are in proportion since the following properties hold:

- The ratio of distance to time $(\frac{D}{t})$ is constant for all values of distance and time. Students can see this if they write different ratios using the data points in the table. For example, $\frac{D}{t} = \frac{3 \text{ yd}}{2 \text{ sec}} = \frac{6 \text{ yd}}{4 \text{ sec}} = \frac{9 \text{ yd}}{6 \text{ sec}}$. (Note: Because of measurement error, experimental data is often not exact; however, the ratios will be approximately equal to one another.)

- The graph of the data is a straight line through the point (0, 0). (Note: In some experiments, due to experimental error, the data points are only close to a straight line.)

- If you multiply one of the variables by a number, the other variable increases by the corresponding factor. For example, if you double the time a student walks, the distance traveled doubles as well.

Students choose among several strategies to solve proportional reasoning problems in the unit. In a science context, the density of an object is defined as the ratio of the object's mass to the object's volume. Students apply concepts of ratio and proportion as they study the density of various materials and discover why some objects sink and others float.

Proportional reasoning is one of the important components of formal thought acquired in adolescence (Hoffer, 1992). This unit builds on concepts and skills involving ratio and proportion that students developed in previous grades and units and uses them as a foundation for more formal thinking. In this way, students have many avenues for solving problems that involve proportional reasoning.

Resources

- Cramer, Kathleen, and Thomas Post. "Making Connections: A Case for Proportionality." *Arithmetic Teacher.* 40 (6), Reston, VA, Feb 1993.

- Hoffer, Alan R., and Shirley Ann K. Hoffer. "Ratios and Proportional Thinking" in *Teaching Mathematics in Grades K–8: Research Based Methods,* Thomas R. Post (ed.). Allyn and Bacon, Boston, MA, 1992.

Observational Assessment Record

A1 Can students use words, tables, graphs, fractions, and colon notation to express ratios?

A2 Can students use ratios and proportions to solve problems?

A3 Can students measure mass?

A4 Can students measure volume by displacement?

A5 Can students collect, organize, graph, and analyze data?

A6 Can students draw and interpret best-fit lines?

A7 Do students solve problems in more than one way?

A8 Can students choose appropriate methods and tools to calculate (calculators, pencil and paper, or mental math)?

A9 _____

Name	A1	A2	A3	A4	A5	A6	A7	A8	A9	Comments
1.										
2.										
3.										
4.										
5.										
6.										
7.										
8.										
9.										
10.										
11.										
12.										

Name	A1	A2	A3	A4	A5	A6	A7	A8	A9	Comments
13.										
14.										
15.										
16.										
17.										
18.										
19.										
20.										
21.										
22.										
23.										
24.										
25.										
26.										
27.										
28.										
29.										
30.										
31.										
32.										

Unit 13

Daily Practice and Problems
Ratio and Proportion

A DPP Menu for Unit 13

Two Daily Practice and Problems (DPP) items are included for each class session listed in the Unit Outline. A scope and sequence chart for the DPP is in the *Teacher Implementation Guide*.

Icons in the Teacher Notes column designate the subject matter of each DPP item. The first item in each class session is always a Bit and the second is either a Task or Challenge. Each item falls into one or more of the categories listed below. A menu of the DPP items for Unit 13 follows.

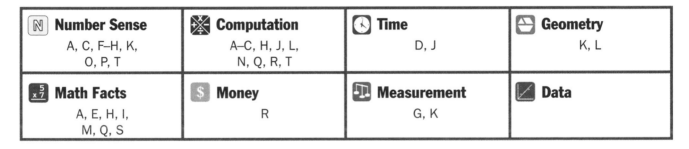

N Number Sense	✖ Computation	🕐 Time	⬡ Geometry
A, C, F–H, K, O, P, T	A–C, H, J, L, N, Q, R, T	D, J	K, L
⁵⁄ₓ₇ Math Facts	$ Money	⚖ Measurement	▨ Data
A, E, H, I, M, Q, S	R	G, K	

The *Daily Practice and Problems and Home Practice Guide* in the *Teacher Implementation Guide* includes information on how and when to use the DPP.

Review of Math Facts

The DPP for this unit continues the systematic approach to reviewing the multiplication and division facts. This unit reviews the facts for the 2s, 5s, 10s, and square numbers. Note: Part 1 of the Home Practice in the *Discovery Assignment Book* provides practice of the facts.

For more information about the distribution and assessment of the math facts, see the TIMS Tutor: *Math Facts* in the *Teacher Implementation Guide*. Also refer to Unit 2 Lesson Guide 2 and the DPP guide in the *Unit Resource Guide* for Unit 2 and the Grade 5 *Facts Resource Guide*. For information about division fact practice throughout second semester, see the DPP guide for Unit 9.

 **Daily Practice and Problems**

Students may solve the items individually, in groups, or as a class. The items may also be assigned for homework. The DPPs are also available on the Teacher Resource CD.

Student Questions	**Teacher Notes**

A **How Square Can You Be?**

Try to do the following in your head.

A. $6^2 \div 4 =$

B. $9^2 \div 9 =$

C. $4^2 \div 8 =$

D. $4^2 \div 2^2 =$

E. $10^2 \div 5^2 =$

F. $8^2 \div 4^2 =$

TIMS Bit

A. 9   B. 9

C. 2   D. 4

E. 4   F. 4

B **Working with Fractions**

All answers should be in lowest terms.

A. $\frac{3}{4} + 1\frac{5}{8} =$

B. $\frac{5}{8} - \frac{1}{2} =$

C. $\frac{3}{8} \times \frac{1}{3} =$

D. $2\frac{2}{3} + 3\frac{4}{9} =$

E. $\frac{8}{9} - \frac{1}{3} =$

F. $\frac{3}{4} \times \frac{2}{3} =$

TIMS Task

A. $2\frac{3}{8}$ B. $\frac{1}{8}$

C. $\frac{1}{8}$ D. $6\frac{1}{9}$

E. $\frac{5}{9}$ F. $\frac{1}{2}$

C **Mental Math**

A. $\frac{1}{2} \times 100 =$

B. $\frac{1}{2} \times 60 =$

C. $\frac{1}{2} \times 80 =$

D. $\frac{1}{2} \times 82 =$

E. $\frac{1}{4} \times 200 =$

F. $\frac{1}{4} \times 80 =$

G. $\frac{1}{6} \times 60 =$

H. $\frac{1}{6} \times 54 =$

TIMS Bit

A. 50   B. 30

C. 40   D. 41

E. 50   F. 20

G. 10   H. 9

(D) Train Rides

Ana's mother takes the train home from work. Today she leaves work at 5:45 P.M. It takes her 5 minutes to walk to the train stop. The first rush hour train arrives at 5:00 P.M. and a train comes every 8 minutes. The train ride is about 25 minutes long. What time should Ana and her father arrive at the train station to pick up Ana's mother?

TIMS Challenge 🕐

She will get to the train stop at 5:50 so she can catch the 5:56 train. Ana and her father should arrive at the train station at about 6:21 P.M.

(E) Practicing the Facts

A. 200 ÷ 40 =

B. 640 ÷ 80 =

C. 400 ÷ 10 =

D. 1200 ÷ 60 =

E. 900 ÷ 90 =

F. 490 ÷ 70 =

G. 8000 ÷ 40 =

H. 40,000 ÷ 80 =

I. 1800 ÷ 20 =

J. 400 ÷ 20 =

TIMS Bit $\frac{5}{\times 7}$

A. 5

B. 8

C. 40

D. 20

E. 10

F. 7

G. 200

H. 500

I. 90

J. 20

F **Speaking of Parts**

Remember that fractions, decimals, and percents are all ways of speaking about parts of a whole. Fill in the chart with equivalent names for the given numbers. Reduce all fractions to lowest terms.

	Fraction	Decimal	Percent
A.		0.10	
B.	$\frac{1}{2}$		
C.			15%
D.		0.4	
E.	$\frac{3}{100}$		
F.			30%
G.	$\frac{3}{4}$		
H.		0.01	

TIMS Task

	Fraction	Decimal	Percent
A.	$\frac{1}{10}$	0.10	10%
B.	$\frac{1}{2}$	0.50 or 0.5	50%
C.	$\frac{3}{20}$	0.15	15%
D.	$\frac{2}{5}$	0.4	40%
E.	$\frac{3}{100}$	0.03	3%
F.	$\frac{3}{10}$	0.30 or 0.3	30%
G.	$\frac{3}{4}$	0.75	75%
H.	$\frac{1}{100}$	0.01	1%

G **Line Segments**

The ratio of the lengths of two line segments is 2:3.

A. If the first line segment is 4 cm long, then what is the length of the second segment? Draw both line segments. Write the length on each segment.

B. If the second segment is 12 cm long, then what is the length of the first segment? Draw both line segments. Write the length on each segment.

TIMS Bit

A. The second segment is 6 cm. One way to solve the problem is to set up a proportion, such as $\frac{2}{3} = \frac{4}{?}$.

B. The first segment is 8 cm. One way to solve the problem is to set up a proportion, such as $\frac{2}{?} = \frac{3}{12}$.

Student Questions	Teacher Notes

(H) Remainders

Solve the following problems. Write the quotients first as whole numbers with remainders, then as mixed numbers, and finally as decimals.

A. $42 \div 5 =$

B. $19 \div 5 =$

C. $7 \div 5 =$

TIMS Task N ⊠ ⊠

A. 8 R2, $8\frac{2}{5}$, 8.4

B. 3 R4, $3\frac{4}{5}$, 3.8

C. 1 R2, $1\frac{2}{5}$, 1.4

Students should have calculators available.

(I) More Facts

Find the value of n that makes these number sentences true.

A. $80 \div 10 = n$

B. $n \div 8 = 2$

C. $30 \div n = 5$

D. $16 \div n = 4$

E. $n \div 9 = 5$

F. $100 \div 10 = n$

G. $100 \div 5 = n$

H. $n \div 3 = 10$

I. $60 \div 2 = n$

J. $9 \div n = 3$

TIMS Bit ⊠

A. 8

B. 16

C. 6

D. 4

E. 45

F. 10

G. 20

H. 30

I. 30

J. 3

J **Founding Fathers**
Who Became Presidents

Founding Father	Birth	Death	President
George Washington	1732	1799	1789–1797
John Adams	1735	1826	1797–1801
Thomas Jefferson	1743	1826	1801–1809
James Madison	1751	1836	1809–1817

A. Which president lived the longest?

B. Who was the youngest of the four presidents when he took office?

C. Which presidents served two terms?

D. How old was Thomas Jefferson when James Madison became president?

E. Madison became president _____ years after Washington's death.

TIMS Task 🕐✖️

A. John Adams at 91 years.

B. George Washington was 57.

C. Washington, Jefferson, and Madison served 8 years which is 2 terms.

D. Jefferson was 66 years old. (1809–1743)

E. 10 years

K **Analogies**

Use the comparison on the left to complete the comparison on the right.

A. 0.5 is to $\frac{1}{2}$ as 0.75 is to _____.

B. Millimeter is to meter as milliliter is to _____.

C. 180° is to triangle as 360° is to _____.

D. Centimeter is to length as square centimeter is to _____.

TIMS Bit 🖐️⚖️ N

There can be other acceptable answers. Common correct answers are given.

A. $\frac{3}{4}$

B. liter

C. quadrilateral (or rectangle or other quadrilateral)

D. area

Student Questions	Teacher Notes

L **Sums of Angles**

A. Draw a triangle with one 50° angle and one 90° angle. What is the measure of the third angle? What is the sum of all three angles?

B. Draw a quadrilateral with one 105° angle and one 90° angle. What are the measures of your other two angles? What is the sum of all four angles?

TIMS Task

A. The third angle should be 40°. The sum of all angles should be 180°.

B. Answers will vary for the measure of the last two angles. The sum of all angles should be 360°.

M **Facts**

Find the value of n that makes these number sentences true.

A. $50 \div 5 = n$

B. $n \div 3 = 5$

C. $36 \div n = 6$

D. $40 \div 20 = n$

E. $700 \div 10 = n$

F. $n \div 5 = 5$

G. $81 \div n = 9$

H. $200 \div 2 = n$

I. $n \div 7 = 2$

J. $35 \div n = 5$

TIMS Bit

A. 10

B. 15

C. 6

D. 2

E. 70

F. 25

G. 9

H. 100

I. 14

J. 7

Student Questions	Teacher Notes

(N) **Working with Large Numbers**

1. Use paper and pencil or mental math to solve the following. Estimate to be sure your answers are reasonable.

   A. $3467 + 9246 =$

   B. $5000 - 4839 =$

   C. $100 \times 2.5 =$

   D. $28{,}468 \div 9 =$

   E. $549 \times 0.3 =$

   F. $13{,}047 \div 28 =$

2. Explain your strategies for Questions 1B and 1C.

TIMS Task ✖

1. A. 12,713
   B. 161
   C. 250
   D. 3163 R1
   E. 164.7
   F. 465 R27

2. Strategies will vary. Possible strategies:

   1B. Count up from 4839 to 5000. $4839 + 1$ is $4840 + 60$ is $4900 + 100$ is 5000. $1 + 60 + 100 = 161$.

   1C. $2 \times 100 = 200$. 0.5 is $\frac{1}{2}$ and $\frac{1}{2}$ of 100 is 50. $200 + 50 = 250$.

(◎) **Making Goop!**

To make enough goop for 4 students to play with, mix 1 part water, 3 parts flour, and 5 parts salt.

If I have:

   A. 8 students, how many parts of salt will I need?

   B. 9 parts flour, how many parts of salt will I need?

   C. 25 parts salt, how many students will have goop?

   D. $\frac{1}{2}$ part water, how many parts of salt and flour do I need?

TIMS Bit [N]

A. 10 parts salt

B. 15 parts salt

C. 20 students

D. $2\frac{1}{2}$ parts salt,

   $1\frac{1}{2}$ parts flour

Student Questions	Teacher Notes

P A Probability Riddle

The answer to this riddle is the name of one of the states of the United States of America. Use these clues to help you determine how many of each letter are in the state's name. Then rearrange the letters to form the name.

The probability of choosing the letter:

O is $\frac{1}{8}$

I is $\frac{3}{8}$

S is $\frac{1}{8}$

L is $\frac{1}{4}$

N is $\frac{1}{8}$

TIMS Challenge N

Since the probability of choosing an O is $\frac{1}{8}$, one of the eight letters is O. There are three I's, one S, two L's, and one N.

Illinois

Students may enjoy making up riddles for other words, including words from their weekly spelling list.

Q Using the Facts

Try to solve the following in your head.

A. $102 \div 10 =$

B. $13 \div 2 =$

C. $39 \div 5 =$

D. $37 \div 6 =$

E. $84 \div 9 =$

F. $63 \div 6 =$

TIMS Bit

A. 10 R2

B. 6 R1

C. 7 R4

D. 6 R1

E. 9 R3

F. 10 R3

Student Questions	Teacher Notes

R Theo the Tutor

A. If Theo earns $10.00 for $2\frac{1}{2}$ hours of tutoring, what is his hourly rate?

B. If Theo needs $57.50 to buy a video game, how many hours will he need to tutor?

C. If Theo tutors 5 hours per week, how much money will he earn after 6 weeks of tutoring?

TIMS Challenge $ ⊠

A. $4.00/hour

B. $57.50 ÷ $4.00 = 14.375, which means he'll need to tutor 15 hours.

C. $120.00

S Division Fact Practice

A. 16 ÷ 8 =   B. 35 ÷ 7 =

C. 49 ÷ 7 =   D. 40 ÷ 10 =

E. 15 ÷ 5 =   F. 16 ÷ 4 =

G. 50 ÷ 5 =   H. 18 ÷ 2 =

I. 70 ÷ 7 =   J. 20 ÷ 10 =

K. 81 ÷ 9 =   L. 64 ÷ 8 =

M. 6 ÷ 2 =   N. 30 ÷ 5 =

O. 100 ÷ 10 =

TIMS Bit $\boxed{\begin{array}{r} 5 \\ \times 7 \end{array}}$

A. 2	B. 5
C. 7	D. 4
E. 3	F. 4
G. 10	H. 9
I. 10	J. 2
K. 9	L. 8
M. 3	N. 6
O. 10	

T Giant Problems

1. Lee Yah is telling a story to her little sister. The story is about a giant and a fifth grader. In the story, bodies of the giant and the fifth grader are proportional. The fifth grader is 140 cm tall and her hand is 12 cm long. If the giant's hand is 36 cm long, how tall is the giant?

2. The giant has three sisters. The first sister is $\frac{5}{6}$ as tall as the giant. The second sister is $\frac{5}{7}$ as tall as the giant. The third sister is $\frac{6}{7}$ as tall as the giant.

   A. Which sister is the tallest?

   B. Calculate the heights of the three sisters.

TIMS Challenge N ✖

1. One strategy students can use is to set up a proportion. $\frac{140 \, cm}{12 \, cm} = \frac{? \, cm}{36 \, cm}$. The giant is 420 cm tall.

2. A. The third sister is the tallest. $\frac{6}{7} > \frac{5}{6} > \frac{5}{7}$

   B. $\frac{6}{7} \times 420$ is 360 cm;

   $\frac{5}{6} \times 420$ is 350 cm;

   $\frac{5}{7} \times 420$ is 300 cm.

Lesson 1

Ratios, Recipes, and Proportions

Estimated Class Sessions

2-3

Lesson Overview

Students review ratios using tables, graphs, and fractions and learn new concepts using recipes as a context. They review writing ratios as fractions and learn to write ratios using colon notation. A proportion is defined as a statement that two ratios are equal. Students then use proportions to solve problems.

Key Content

- Using numerical variables.
- Using words, tables, graphs, and fractions to express ratios.
- Translating between different representations of ratios (graphical and symbolic).
- Using ratios and proportions to solve problems.
- Drawing and interpreting best-fit lines.
- Using patterns in data tables and graphs to solve problems.

Key Vocabulary

- extrapolation
- interpolation
- proportion
- ratio
- unit ratio

Math Facts

DPP Bit A reviews division facts for the square numbers.

Homework

1. Assign the Homework section in the *Student Guide.*
2. Assign Parts 1–2 of the Home Practice.

Assessment

1. Use *Questions 21–23* of the Peanut Cake section in the *Student Guide* to assess students' abilities to write ratios and use proportions.
2. Assign Part 5 of the Home Practice to assess students' fluency in solving problems involving ratio and proportion.
3. Use the *Observational Assessment Record* to note students' abilities to use words, tables, graphs, fractions, and colon notation to express ratios.

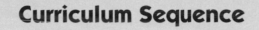

Curriculum Sequence

Before This Unit

Ratios

In Unit 3 Lesson 5 students used words, tables, graphs, and fractions to express ratios. They found equal ratios and used them to solve problems. They also used ratios to solve problems in the labs *Distance vs. Time* in Unit 3, *Spreading Out* in Unit 4, and *A Day at the Races* in Unit 5.

Interpolation and Extrapolation

Students were introduced to the terms interpolation and extrapolation in Grade 4 Unit 5 Lesson 1 *Predictions from Graphs*. They continued to use the terms in the labs throughout fourth grade.

George Washington Carver

In fifth grade, the Adventure Books *George Washington Carver: A Man of Measure* in Unit 4 and *Peanut Soup* in Unit 12 tell about the work of George Washington Carver at Tuskegee Institute.

After This Unit

Ratios

Students will use ratios to develop the formula for the circumference of a circle in the lab *Circumference vs. Diameter* in Unit 14 and use proportions to solve problems in the lab *How Many Bats in a Cave?* in Unit 16.

Interpolation and Extrapolation

Students will use interpolation and extrapolation in the labs in Units 14 and 16

Materials List

Supplies and Copies

Student	Teacher
Supplies for Each Student • calculator	**Supplies**
Copies • 1 copy of *Centimeter Graph Paper* per student (*Unit Resource Guide* Page 34)	**Copies/Transparencies** • 1 copy of *Observational Assessment Record* to be used throughout this unit (*Unit Resource Guide* Pages 11–12) • 1 transparency of *Centimeter Graph Paper* (*Unit Resource Guide* Page 34)

All blackline masters including assessment, transparency, and DPP masters are also on the Teacher Resource CD.

Student Books

Ratios, Recipes, and Proportions (*Student Guide* Pages 396–401)

Daily Practice and Problems and Home Practice

DPP items A–D (*Unit Resource Guide* Pages 14–15)
Home Practice Parts 1–2 & 5 (*Discovery Assignment Book* Pages 201–202 & 204)

Note: Classrooms whose pacing differs significantly from the suggested pacing of the units should use the Math Facts Calendar in Section 4 of the *Facts Resource Guide* to ensure students receive the complete math facts program.

Assessment Tools

Observational Assessment Record (*Unit Resource Guide* Pages 11–12)

Daily Practice and Problems

Suggestions for using the DPPs are on page 31.

A. Bit: How Square Can You Be? $\boxed{N}$ $\boxed{⊠}$ $\boxed{\frac{5}{\times 7}}$
(URG p. 14)

Try to do the following in your head.

A. $6^2 \div 4 =$ B. $9^2 \div 9 =$

C. $4^2 \div 8 =$ D. $4^2 \div 2^2 =$

E. $10^2 \div 5^2 =$ F. $8^2 \div 4^2 =$

C. Bit: Mental Math (URG p. 14) $\boxed{N}$ $\boxed{⊠}$

A. $\frac{1}{2} \times 100 =$ B. $\frac{1}{2} \times 60 =$

C. $\frac{1}{2} \times 80 =$ D. $\frac{1}{2} \times 82 =$

E. $\frac{1}{4} \times 200 =$ F. $\frac{1}{4} \times 80 =$

G. $\frac{1}{6} \times 60 =$ H. $\frac{1}{6} \times 54 =$

B. Task: Working with Fractions $\boxed{⊠}$
(URG p. 14)

All answers should be in lowest terms.

A. $\frac{3}{4} + 1\frac{5}{8} =$ B. $\frac{5}{8} - \frac{1}{2} =$

C. $\frac{3}{8} \times \frac{1}{3} =$ D. $2\frac{2}{3} + 3\frac{4}{9} =$

E. $\frac{8}{9} - \frac{1}{3} =$ F. $\frac{3}{4} \times \frac{2}{3} =$

D. Challenge: Train Rides (URG p. 15) $\boxed{🕐}$

Ana's mother takes the train home from work. Today she leaves work at 5:45 P.M. It takes her 5 minutes to walk to the train stop. The first rush hour train arrives at 5:00 P.M. and a train comes every 8 minutes. The train ride is about 25 minutes long. What time should Ana and her father arrive at the train station to pick up Ana's mother?

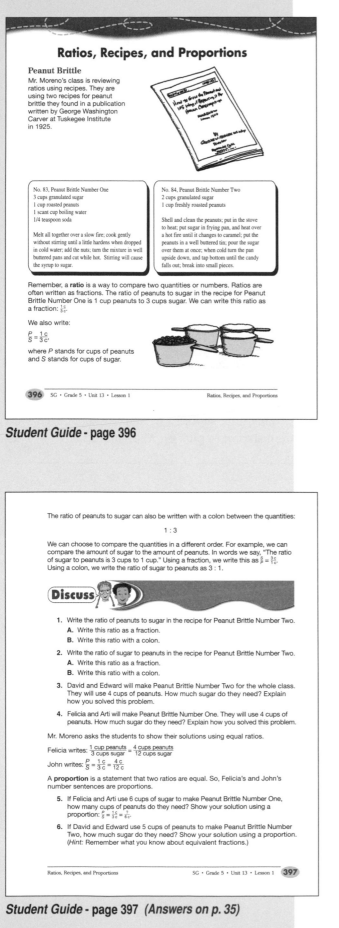

Student Guide - page 396

Student Guide - page 397 (Answers on p. 35)

Teaching the Activity

Part 1 Peanut Brittle: Ratio and Proportion

Begin by reading the Peanut Brittle section in the *Student Guide*. **Questions 1–2** ask students to write ratios using two different types of notation. For example, the ratio of peanuts to sugar in a peanut brittle recipe is 1 cup peanuts to 2 cups sugar. Students write this ratio as $\frac{1\,c}{2\,c}$ and also as 1 : 2. They use the ratios to solve problems in **Questions 3–4.** Discuss students' strategies. Two possible strategies are using multiplication and using equal ratios.

> ### Content Note
>
> **Colon Notation.** Since ratios are sometimes written using colon notation, we introduce it here so students will recognize ratios written this way. However, we will more often write ratios as fractions since this notation is usually easier to use when solving problems.

In solving these ratio problems students need to keep track of which ratio they are writing:

cups of peanuts : cups of sugar, or

cups of sugar : cups of peanuts.

One way to do this is to use the units. In other words, write $\frac{1 \text{ cup peanuts}}{2 \text{ cups sugar}}$. Another method is to use variables, for example, the letter P for cups of peanuts and S for cups of sugar. Then, we write, $\frac{P}{S} = \frac{1\,c}{2\,c}$. Remind students that this equation is just a shorthand way of saying "the ratio of cups of peanuts to cups of sugar is 1 cup to 2 cups." This is the way ratios are usually written in *Math Trailblazers*.

Questions 5–6 introduce the term **proportion** as a statement of equality between ratios. These questions encourage students to use what they have learned about equal ratios to solve problems involving the ratios in two peanut brittle recipes. For example, to solve **Question 6,** students refer to a recipe that calls for 1 cup peanuts and 2 cups sugar. They must find the number of cups of sugar to mix with 5 cups of peanuts. Students can use either of these proportions:

$$\frac{P}{S} = \frac{1\,c}{2\,c} = \frac{5\,c}{?} \qquad\qquad \frac{S}{P} = \frac{2\,c}{1\,c} = \frac{?}{5\,c}$$

$$\frac{1\,c}{2\,c} = \frac{5\,c}{10\,c} \qquad\qquad \frac{2\,c}{1\,c} = \frac{10\,c}{5\,c}$$

So the amount of sugar is 10 cups.

They can solve the proportions using the same strategies and procedures they have used to find equivalent fractions.

Part 2 Orange Punch: Ratios, Proportions, and Graphs

In *Questions 7–20* students express the ratio 5 cups juice to 2 cups soda using a table, graph, and symbols. They use these tools to solve proportional reasoning problems. *Question 8* asks what patterns they see in the table in Figure 2. Students may say that the number of cups of soda and of juice double as you move down the columns. Also, the numbers of cups of soda are all multiples of 2 and the numbers of cups of juice are all multiples of 5.

Orange Punch

S Lime Soda (in cups)	J Orange Juice (in cups)
2	5
4	10
8	20

Figure 2: *Table showing ratios equal to 5 c orange juice/2 c lime soda*

In *Question 9,* students use the ratios in the table to write proportions and solve problems.

In *Question 10* students make a graph by plotting the number of cups of soda on the horizontal axis and the number of cups of juice on the vertical axis. A point graph is appropriate since it makes sense to talk about points in between the data points in the table. For example, if we plot points and fit a line as shown in Figure 3, we can use the graph to find the number of cups of juice to mix with 6 cups of soda.

The graph is a straight line that goes uphill. *(Question 11)* It meets the vertical axis at the point (0 c, 0 c). Students use the graph to solve proportional reasoning problems in *Question 12* and show their work on the graph as shown in Figure 3.

Question 13 reviews the terms **interpolation** and **extrapolation.** Using the graph to make predictions with points that lie between the plotted data is called interpolation. Using points beyond the range of the plotted data is called extrapolation.

Orange Punch
Shannon plans to make punch using a family recipe. She mixes 5 parts orange juice with 2 parts lime soda. For example, if she uses 5 cups of orange juice, she uses 2 cups of lime soda. Shannon makes a chart so that the other members of the class can help her make different amounts of punch.

S Lime Soda (in cups)	J Orange Juice (in cups)
2	5
4	10
8	20

7. A. Write the ratio of orange juice to lime soda with a colon.
    B. Write this ratio as a fraction.

8. Describe any patterns you see in the table.

9. A. If Shannon uses 4 cups of lime soda, how many cups of orange juice does she use? Write your solution as a proportion: $\frac{J}{S} = \frac{5c}{2c} = \frac{7c}{4c}$.
    B. If Shannon uses 20 cups of orange juice, how many cups of lime soda does she use? Write your solution as a proportion.

10. Shannon can also use a graph to help her make different amounts of punch. Make a graph of the data in the table.
    • Plot the amount of lime soda on the horizontal axis. Scale the horizontal axis from 0 to at least 30.
    • Plot the amount of orange juice on the vertical axis. Scale the vertical axis from 0 to at least 40.
    • Will you use a point graph or a bar graph? (*Hint:* You will want to find points in between the data.)
    • If you graph points that form a line, use your ruler to fit a line to the points. Extend your line in both directions.

11. Describe your graph. (Where does it meet the vertical axis? Is it a straight line or a curve? Does it go up or down as you read from left to right?)

Student Guide - page 398 *(Answers on p. 35)*

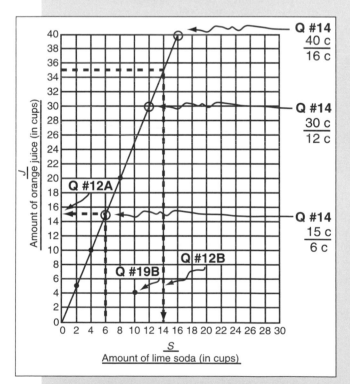

Figure 3: *Sample graph for* **Question 10**

12. **A.** Use your graph to find the number of cups of orange juice to mix with 6 cups of lime soda.
    B. Use your graph to find the number of cups of lime soda to mix with 35 cups of orange juice.

Using the graph to find an amount of soda or juice that lies *between* two data points you plotted on the graph is called **interpolation.** "Inter" means between points.

Using the graph to find an amount of soda or juice that lies *beyond* the points you plotted on the graph is called **extrapolation.** "Extra" means beyond or outside.

13. **A.** Did you use interpolation or extrapolation to answer Question 12A?
    B. Did you use interpolation or extrapolation to answer Question 12B?

14. **A.** Choose a point on the line and circle it. Use this point to write a ratio of the amount of orange juice to the amount of lime soda.
    B. Circle two more points on the line. Use them to write ratios of the amount of orange juice to the amount of lime soda.
    C. Are the three ratios equal? How do you know?

15. **A.** Find the number of cups of lime soda to mix with 25 cups of orange juice. How did you solve this problem?
    B. One way to solve this problem is to use a proportion. Find ? so that the number sentence is true. $\frac{J}{S} = \frac{5\,c}{2\,c} = \frac{25\,c}{?}$

16. **A.** Use a proportion to find the number of cups of orange juice to mix with 18 cups of lime soda.
    B. Use a proportion to find the number of cups of lime soda to mix with 55 cups of orange juice.

Unit Ratios

17. Find the number of cups of orange juice to mix with 1 cup of lime soda.

A **unit ratio** is a ratio in which the denominator is one. For example, $\frac{J}{S} = \frac{2.5\,c}{1\,c}$ is a unit ratio. You can use unit ratios to help you solve problems. To find the number of cups of orange juice to mix with 3 cups of lime soda, multiply 2.5×3 to get 7.5 cups of orange juice.

18. Find the number of cups of orange juice to mix with 7 cups of lime soda. Show how you solved this problem.

19. Shannon's little sister mixed 4 cups of orange juice with 10 cups of lime soda. When Shannon drank the punch, she thought it tasted funny.
    A. Why did the punch taste different from the usual recipe?
    B. Plot a point for 10 cups of lime soda and 4 cups of orange juice on your graph. Does the point lie on the line?

20. **A.** If Shannon follows the recipe and uses 5 cups of orange juice, how many total cups of punch will she make?
    B. Write a ratio comparing the number of cups of orange juice to the total number of cups of punch.

Peanut Cake

Jessie and Jackie will make peanut cakes for the whole class:

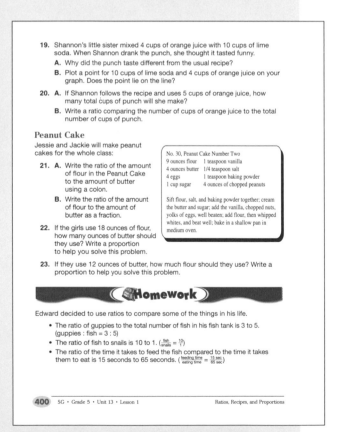

No. 30, Peanut Cake Number Two
9 ounces flour   1 teaspoon vanilla
4 ounces butter   1/4 teaspoon salt
4 eggs   1 teaspoon baking powder
1 cup sugar   4 ounces of chopped peanuts

Sift flour, salt, and baking powder together; cream the butter and sugar; add the vanilla, chopped nuts, yolks of eggs, well beaten; add flour, then whipped whites, and beat well; bake in a shallow pan in medium oven.

21. **A.** Write the ratio of the amount of flour in the Peanut Cake to the amount of butter using a colon.
    B. Write the ratio of the amount of flour to the amount of butter as a fraction.

22. If the girls use 18 ounces of flour, how many ounces of butter should they use? Write a proportion to help you solve this problem.

23. If they use 12 ounces of butter, how much flour should they use? Write a proportion to help you solve this problem.

(Homework)

Edward decided to use ratios to compare some of the things in his life.

- The ratio of guppies to the total number of fish in his fish tank is 3 to 5. (guppies : fish = 3 : 5)
- The ratio of fish to snails is 10 to 1. ($\frac{fish}{snails} = \frac{10}{1}$)
- The ratio of the time it takes to feed the fish compared to the time it takes them to eat is 15 seconds to 65 seconds. ($\frac{feeding\ time}{eating\ time} = \frac{15\ sec}{65\ sec}$)

For **Question 14** students choose three points on the line and use them to write ratios comparing the amount of juice to the amount of soda. Three possible points are circled on the graph in Figure 3. The ratios for these points are below. The three ratios are equal since they all reduce to $\frac{5\,c}{2\,c}$.

$$\frac{15\,c}{6\,c} = \frac{5\,c}{2\,c} \qquad \frac{30\,c}{12\,c} = \frac{5\,c}{2\,c} \qquad \frac{40\,c}{16\,c} = \frac{5\,c}{2\,c}$$

Students can use many strategies to solve the problem in **Question 15.** They must find the number of cups of soda to mix with 25 c of juice. They can use the graph or use the patterns in the table. **Question 15B,** however, asks students to use a proportion to solve the problem. Encourage students to use what they know about equivalent fractions.

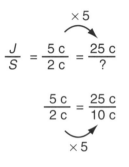

$$\frac{J}{S} = \frac{5\,c}{2\,c} = \frac{25\,c}{?}$$

$$\frac{5\,c}{2\,c} = \frac{25\,c}{10\,c}$$

Since $5 \times 5 = 25$, we can multiply 2×5 to get 10 cups of soda. Note that we don't ask students to follow a specific procedure to solve the proportion. Instead we prefer students to solve proportions by relying on their previous knowledge of equivalent fractions. Of course, there are other methods for solving this problem. Students practice using proportions in **Question 16.**

Question 17 asks students to find the number of cups of orange juice to mix with 1 cup of lime soda. They can use division ($5 \div 2$) to find that $2\frac{1}{2}$ cups (or 2.5 cups) of juice are needed for each cup of soda. We can write this as a ratio with a denominator of one ($\frac{2.5\,c}{1\,c}$). This is called a **unit ratio** and can be used to solve other problems. For example, **Question 18** asks students to find the number of cups of juice to mix with 7 cups of soda. Students can use calculators to multiply: $7 \times 2.5 = 17.5$ cups of juice.

In **Question 19** students add the point (10 c, 4 c) to their graphs. See Figure 3. This point does not lie on the line, since the ratio corresponding to this point ($\frac{J}{S} = \frac{4\,c}{10\,c}$) is not equal to $\frac{5\,c}{2\,c}$. Since Shannon's little sister did not use the ingredients in the same proportion as Shannon, the punch will not taste the same.

Question 20 asks students to write the ratio of the number of cups of orange juice to the total number of cups of punch. If Shannon uses 5 cups of orange juice, she will use 2 cups of lime soda and make 7 cups of punch. So the ratio of orange juice to punch is $\frac{5\,c}{7\,c}$.

Math Facts

DPP item A reviews division facts for square numbers.

Homework and Practice

- Assign the problems in the Homework section of the *Student Guide.*

- Assign DPP items B and C, which review computation with fractions. Challenge D is a problem involving elapsed time.

- Assign Parts 1 and 2 of the Home Practice.

Assessment

- Use **Questions 21–23** of the Peanut Cake section in the *Student Guide* to assess students' abilities to write ratios and use proportions to solve problems.

- Use Home Practice Part 5 to assess students' understanding of ratio and proportion.

- Use the *Observational Assessment Record* to note students' abilities to express ratios using words, tables, graphs, fractions, and colon notation.

Answers for Parts 1, 2, and 5 of the Home Practice are in the Answer Key at the end of this lesson and at the end of this unit.

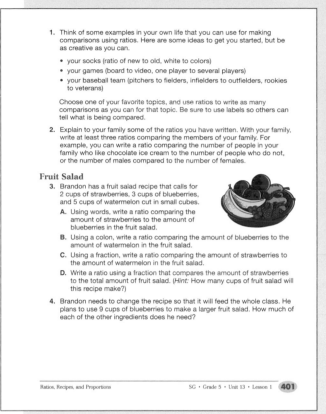

1. Think of some examples in your own life that you can use for making comparisons using ratios. Here are some ideas to get you started, but be as creative as you can.

   - your socks (ratio of new to old, white to colors)
   - your games (board to video, one player to several players)
   - your baseball team (pitchers to fielders, infielders to outfielders, rookies to veterans)

   Choose one of your favorite topics, and use ratios to write as many comparisons as you can for that topic. Be sure to use labels so others can tell what is being compared.

2. Explain to your family some of the ratios you have written. With your family, write at least three ratios comparing the members of your family. For example, you can write a ratio comparing the number of people in your family who like chocolate ice cream to the number of people who do not, or the number of males compared to the number of females.

Fruit Salad

3. Brandon has a fruit salad recipe that calls for 2 cups of strawberries, 3 cups of blueberries, and 5 cups of watermelon cut in small cubes.

   A. Using words, write a ratio comparing the amount of strawberries to the amount of blueberries in the fruit salad.

   B. Using a colon, write a ratio comparing the amount of blueberries to the amount of watermelon in the fruit salad.

   C. Using a fraction, write a ratio comparing the amount of strawberries to the amount of watermelon in the fruit salad.

   D. Write a ratio using a fraction that compares the amount of strawberries to the total amount of fruit salad. (*Hint:* How many cups of fruit salad will this recipe make?)

4. Brandon needs to change the recipe so that it will feed the whole class. He plans to use 9 cups of blueberries to make a larger fruit salad. How much of each of the other ingredients does he need?

Ratios, Recipes, and Proportions   SG • Grade 5 • Unit 13 • Lesson 1   **401**

Student Guide - page 401 (Answers on p. 37)

Name _____ Date _____

Unit 13 Home Practice

PART 1   **Division Practice**

A. $45 \div 9 =$	B. $4 \div 2 =$	C. $10 \div 5 =$
D. $9 \div 3 =$	E. $60 \div 6 =$	F. $25 \div 5 =$
G. $40 \div 5 =$	H. $36 \div 6 =$	I. $30 \div 10 =$
J. $8 \div 4 =$	K. $20 \div 4 =$	L. $12 \div 6 =$
M. $80 \div 8 =$	N. $14 \div 2 =$	O. $90 \div 10 =$

PART 2   **Fractions, Decimals, and Percents**

1. Find n to make each pair of fractions equivalent.

   A. $\frac{4}{5} = \frac{n}{20}$ B. $\frac{9}{10} = \frac{36}{n}$ C. $\frac{4}{n} = \frac{28}{49}$

   D. $\frac{n}{8} = \frac{4}{32}$ E. $\frac{5}{6} = \frac{n}{36}$ F. $\frac{3}{4} = \frac{60}{n}$

RATIO AND PROPORTION   DAB • Grade 5 • Unit 13 **201**

Discovery Assignment Book - page 201 (Answers on p. 37)

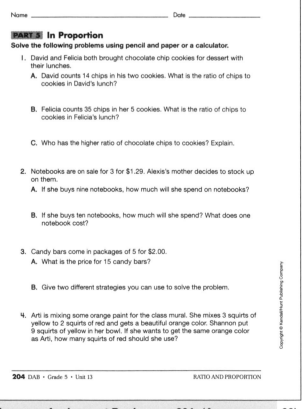

Name _____ **Date** _____

2. For each pair of numbers write a number sentence using <, >, and =.
(*Hint:* Use a calculator to change the fractions to decimals.)

A. $\frac{1}{6}$ and 30%   B. 65% and $\frac{5}{8}$ C. $\frac{4}{9}$ and 46%

D. 0.66 and $\frac{2}{3}$ E. 0.43 and $\frac{3}{7}$ F. $\frac{6}{15}$ and 40%

PART 3 Computation Practice

Solve the following problems using paper and pencil. Estimate to be sure your answers are reasonable. Give your answers to division problems as mixed numbers. Use a separate sheet of paper if you need more space.

A. $87 \times 62 =$ B. $2.3 \times 52 =$ C. $1892 \div 5 =$

D. $3406 \div 27 =$ E. $4\frac{5}{6} + 3\frac{1}{5} =$ F. $\frac{11}{12} + 1\frac{2}{3} =$

G. $\frac{2}{3} \times 36 =$ H. $\frac{3}{5} \times \frac{5}{6} =$ I. $314.56 + .89 =$

J. $1089.23 - 17.9 =$ K. $58 - .36 =$ L. $173.4 + 38.65 =$

202 DAB • Grade 5 • Unit 13   RATIO AND PROPORTION

Discovery Assignment Book - **page 202** *(Answers on p. 38)*

Name _____ **Date** _____

PART 5 In Proportion

Solve the following problems using pencil and paper or a calculator.

1. David and Felicia both brought chocolate chip cookies for dessert with their lunches.
   A. David counts 14 chips in his two cookies. What is the ratio of chips to cookies in David's lunch?

   B. Felicia counts 35 chips in her 5 cookies. What is the ratio of chips to cookies in Felicia's lunch?

   C. Who has the higher ratio of chocolate chips to cookies? Explain.

2. Notebooks are on sale for 3 for $1.29. Alexis's mother decides to stock up on them.
   A. If she buys nine notebooks, how much will she spend on notebooks?

   B. If she buys ten notebooks, how much will she spend? What does one notebook cost?

3. Candy bars come in packages of 5 for $2.00.
   A. What is the price for 15 candy bars?

   B. Give two different strategies you can use to solve the problem.

4. Arti is mixing some orange paint for the class mural. She mixes 3 squirts of yellow to 2 squirts of red and gets a beautiful orange color. Shannon put 9 squirts of yellow in her bowl. If she wants to get the same orange color as Arti, how many squirts of red should she use?

204 DAB • Grade 5 • Unit 13   RATIO AND PROPORTION

Discovery Assignment Book - **page 204** *(Answers on p. 38)*

Literature Connection

Carter, Andy, and Carol Saller. *George Washington Carver.* Carolrhoda Books, Inc. Minneapolis, MN, 2001.

Resources

Carver, George Washington. *How to Grow the Peanut and 105 Ways of Preparing It for Human Consumption.* Seventh Edition. Tuskegee Institute, Tuskegee, AL, January, 1940.

Estimated Class Sessions **2-3**

At a Glance

Math Facts and Daily Practice and Problems

Assign DPP items A–D. Bit A reviews division facts for the square numbers. Items B and C review fractions. Challenge D offers a time problem.

Part 1. Peanut Brittle: Ratio and Proportion

1. Review ratios and introduce colon notation using *Questions 1–4* on the *Ratios, Recipes, and Proportions* Activity Pages in the *Student Guide.*
2. Define proportion using *Questions 5–6.*

Part 2. Orange Punch: Ratios, Proportions, and Graphs

1. Students review using data tables and graphs to represent ratios and investigate connections between graphs and proportional reasoning. *(Questions 7–16 and 19)*
2. Students find and use unit ratios to solve problems. *(Questions 17–18)*
3. Students practice writing ratios and using proportions in *Questions 20–23.*

Homework

1. Assign the Homework section in the *Student Guide.*
2. Assign Parts 1–2 of the Home Practice.

Assessment

1. Use *Questions 21–23* of the Peanut Cake section in the *Student Guide* to assess students' abilities to write ratios and use proportions.
2. Assign Part 5 of the Home Practice to assess students' fluency in solving problems involving ratio and proportion.
3. Use the *Observational Assessment Record* to note students' abilities to use words, tables, graphs, fractions, and colon notation to express ratios.

Connection

Read and discuss *George Washington Carver* by Andy Carter and Carol Saller.

Answer Key is on pages 35–38.

Notes:

Name _____ Date _____

Centimeter Graph Paper, Blackline Master

Student Guide (p. 397)

1. A. $\frac{1\,c}{2\,c}$

   B. 1 cup peanuts : 2 cups sugar

2. A. $\frac{2\,c}{1\,c}$

   B. 2 cups sugar : 1 cup peanuts

3. 8 cups sugar. There is always twice as much sugar as peanuts.

4. 12 cups sugar. There is always three times as much sugar as peanuts.

5. 2 cups; $\frac{1\,c}{3\,c} = \frac{2\,c}{6\,c}$

6. 10 cups sugar; $\frac{1\,c}{2\,c} = \frac{5\,c}{10\,c}$*

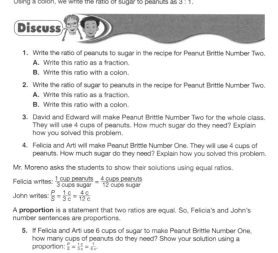

The ratio of peanuts to sugar can also be written with a colon between the quantities:

1 : 3

We can choose to compare the quantities in a different order. For example, we can compare the amount of sugar to the amount of peanuts. In words we say, "The ratio of sugar to peanuts is 3 cups to 1 cup." Using a fraction, we write this as $\frac{S}{P} = \frac{3\,c}{1\,c}$. Using a colon, we write the ratio of sugar to peanuts as 3 : 1.

Discuss

1. Write the ratio of peanuts to sugar in the recipe for Peanut Brittle Number Two.
   A. Write this ratio as a fraction.
   B. Write this ratio with a colon.

2. Write the ratio of sugar to peanuts in the recipe for Peanut Brittle Number Two.
   A. Write this ratio as a fraction.
   B. Write this ratio with a colon.

3. David and Edward will make Peanut Brittle Number Two for the whole class. They will use 4 cups of peanuts. How much sugar do they need? Explain how you solved this problem.

4. Felicia and Arti will make Peanut Brittle Number One. They will use 4 cups of peanuts. How much sugar do they need? Explain how you solved this problem.

Mr. Moreno asks the students to show their solutions using equal ratios.

Felicia writes: $\frac{1\text{ cup peanuts}}{3\text{ cups sugar}} = \frac{4\text{ cups peanuts}}{12\text{ cups sugar}}$

John writes: $\frac{P}{S} = \frac{1\,c}{3\,c} = \frac{4\,c}{12\,c}$

A **proportion** is a statement that two ratios are equal. So, Felicia's and John's number sentences are proportions.

5. If Felicia and Arti use 6 cups of sugar to make Peanut Brittle Number One, how many cups of peanuts do they need? Show your solution using a proportion: $\frac{P}{S} = \frac{1\,c}{3\,c} = \frac{?}{6\,c}$.

6. If David and Edward use 5 cups of peanuts to make Peanut Brittle Number Two, how much sugar do they need? Show your solution using a proportion. (*Hint*: Remember what you know about equivalent fractions.)

Ratios, Recipes, and Proportions   SG • Grade 5 • Unit 13 • Lesson 1   **397**

Student Guide - page 397

Student Guide (p. 398)

7. A. 5 c orange juice : 2 c lime soda

   B. $\frac{5\text{ c orange juice}}{2\text{ c lime soda}}$

8. Answers may vary. Possible responses include: As you double the number of cups of lime soda, you double the orange juice. The numbers of cups of lime soda are all multiples of 2 and the numbers of cups of orange juice are all multiples of 5.

9. A. 10 cups; $\frac{J}{S} = \frac{5\,c}{2\,c} = \frac{10\,c}{4\,c}$

   B. 8 cups; $\frac{J}{S} = \frac{5\,c}{2\,c} = \frac{20\,c}{8\,c}$

10. The graph is a point graph. See Figure 3 in the Lesson Guide.*

11. The graph is a straight line that goes up as we read from left to right and it meets the vertical axis at the point (0, 0).*

Orange Punch

Shannon plans to make punch using a family recipe. She mixes 5 parts orange juice with 2 parts lime soda. For example, if she uses 5 cups of orange juice, she uses 2 cups of lime soda. Shannon makes a chart so that the other members of the class can help her make different amounts of punch.

S Lime Soda (in cups)	J Orange Juice (in cups)
2	5
4	10
8	20

7. A. Write the ratio of orange juice to lime soda with a colon.
   B. Write this ratio as a fraction.

8. Describe any patterns you see in the table.

9. A. If Shannon uses 4 cups of lime soda, how many cups of orange juice does she use? Write your solution as a proportion: $\frac{J}{S} = \frac{5\,c}{2\,c} = \frac{?}{4\,c}$.
   B. If Shannon uses 20 cups of orange juice, how many cups of lime soda does she use? Write your solution as a proportion.

10. Shannon can also use a graph to help her make different amounts of punch. Make a graph of the data in the table.
    • Plot the amount of lime soda on the horizontal axis. Scale the horizontal axis from 0 to at least 30.
    • Plot the amount of orange juice on the vertical axis. Scale the vertical axis from 0 to at least 40.
    • Will you use a point graph or a bar graph? (*Hint*: You will want to find points in between the data.)
    • If you graph points that form a line, use your ruler to fit a line to the points. Extend your line in both directions.

11. Describe your graph. (Where does it meet the vertical axis? Is it a straight line or a curve? Does it go up or down as you read from left to right?)

398   SG • Grade 5 • Unit 13 • Lesson 1   Ratios, Recipes, and Proportions

Student Guide - page 398

*Answers and/or discussion are included in the Lesson Guide.

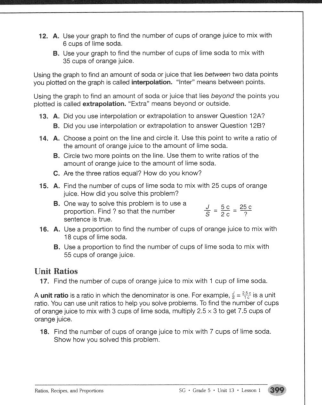

Student Guide - page 399

Student Guide (p. 399)

12.* **A.** 15 cups. See Figure 3 in Lesson Guide 1.

B. 14 cups. See Figure 3 in Lesson Guide 1.

13.* **A.** Interpolation

B. Extrapolation

14. **A.–B.*** See Figure 3 in Lesson Guide 1.

C. Yes. The three ratios are all equal since they all reduce to $\frac{5\,c}{2\,c}$.

15.* **A.** 10 cups. Students can use the graph, the patterns in the table, or equal ratios.

B. $\frac{J}{S} = \frac{5\,c}{2\,c} = \frac{25\,c}{10\,c}$

16. **A.** 45 cups; $\frac{J}{S} = \frac{5\,c}{2\,c} = \frac{?}{18\,c}$; $? = 45\,c$

B. 22 cups; $\frac{J}{S} = \frac{5\,c}{2\,c} = \frac{55c}{?}$; $? = 22\,c$

17. $2\frac{1}{2}$ cups; $5 \div 2 = 2\frac{1}{2}$*

18. $17\frac{1}{2}$ cups; $2\frac{1}{2} \times 7 = 17\frac{1}{2}$

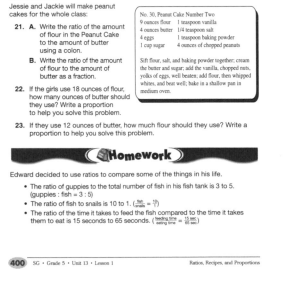

Student Guide - page 400

Student Guide (p. 400)

19.* **A.** The ratio, $\frac{J}{S} = \frac{4\,c}{10\,c}$, is not equal to $\frac{5\,c}{2\,c}$. Since Shannon's sister did not use the ingredients in the same proportion as Shannon, the punch will not taste the same. She was supposed to use 25 cups of orange juice with 10 cups of lime soda for the usual recipe.

B. The point does not lie on the line. See Figure 3 in Lesson Guide 1.

20. **A.** 7 cups

B. $\frac{\text{amount of orange juice}}{\text{total amount of punch}} = \frac{5\,c}{7\,c}$

21. **A.** 9 ounces of flour : 4 ounces of butter*

B. $\frac{9 \text{ ounces}}{4 \text{ ounces}}$

22. 8 ounces; $\frac{F}{B} = \frac{9 \text{ ounces}}{4 \text{ ounces}} = \frac{18 \text{ ounces}}{?}$; $? = 8$ ounces

23. 27 ounces; $\frac{F}{B} = \frac{9 \text{ ounces}}{4 \text{ ounces}} = \frac{?}{12 \text{ ounces}}$; $? = 27$ ounces

*Answers and/or discussion are included in the Lesson Guide.

Student Guide (p. 401)

Homework

1. Answers will vary.

2. Answers will vary.

3. **A.** The ratio of the amount of strawberries to the amount of blueberries is 2 cups to 3 cups.

   B. 3 cups of blueberries : 5 cups of watermelon

   C. 2 cups of strawberries : 5 cups of watermelon

   D. $\frac{2 \text{ cups of strawberries}}{10 \text{ cups of fruit salad}}$

4. 6 cups of strawberries and 15 cups of watermelon; $\frac{S}{B} = \frac{2}{3} = \frac{?}{9}$; $\frac{W}{B} = \frac{5}{3} = \frac{?}{9}$

1. Think of some examples in your own life that you can use for making comparisons using ratios. Here are some ideas to get you started, but be as creative as you can.

   • your socks (ratio of new to old, white to colors)
   • your games (board to video, one player to several players)
   • your baseball team (pitchers to fielders, infielders to outfielders, rookies to veterans)

   Choose one of your favorite topics, and use ratios to write as many comparisons as you can for that topic. Be sure to use labels so others can tell what is being compared.

2. Explain to your family some of the ratios you have written. With your family, write at least three ratios comparing the members of your family. For example, you can write a ratio comparing the number of people in your family who like chocolate ice cream to the number of people who do not, or the number of males compared to the number of females.

Fruit Salad

3. Brandon has a fruit salad recipe that calls for 2 cups of strawberries, 3 cups of blueberries, and 5 cups of watermelon cut in small cubes.

   A. Using words, write a ratio comparing the amount of strawberries to the amount of blueberries in the fruit salad.

   B. Using a colon, write a ratio comparing the amount of blueberries to the amount of watermelon in the fruit salad.

   C. Using a fraction, write a ratio comparing the amount of strawberries to the amount of watermelon in the fruit salad.

   D. Write a ratio using a fraction that compares the amount of strawberries to the total amount of fruit salad. (*Hint:* How many cups of fruit salad will this recipe make?)

4. Brandon needs to change the recipe so that it will feed the whole class. He plans to use 9 cups of blueberries to make a larger fruit salad. How much of each of the other ingredients does he need?

Ratios, Recipes, and Proportions   SG • Grade 5 • Unit 13 • Lesson 1   **401**

Student Guide - page 401

Discovery Assignment Book (p. 201)

Home Practice*

Part 1. Division Practice

A. 5	**B.** 2
C. 2	**D.** 3
E. 10	**F.** 5
G. 8	**H.** 6
I. 3	**J.** 2
K. 5	**L.** 2
M. 10	**N.** 7
O. 9	

Part 2. Fractions, Decimals, and Percents

1. **A.** 16; $\frac{4}{5} = \frac{16}{20}$

   B. 40; $\frac{9}{10} = \frac{36}{40}$

   C. 7; $\frac{4}{7} = \frac{28}{49}$

   D. 1; $\frac{1}{8} = \frac{4}{32}$

   E. 30; $\frac{5}{6} = \frac{30}{36}$

   F. 80; $\frac{3}{4} = \frac{60}{80}$

Name _____ Date _____

Unit 13 Home Practice

PART 1 Division Practice

A. $45 \div 9 =$	**B.** $4 \div 2 =$	**C.** $10 \div 5 =$
D. $9 \div 3 =$	**E.** $60 \div 6 =$	**F.** $25 \div 5 =$
G. $40 \div 5 =$	**H.** $36 \div 6 =$	**I.** $30 \div 10 =$
J. $8 \div 4 =$	**K.** $20 \div 4 =$	**L.** $12 \div 6 =$
M. $80 \div 8 =$	**N.** $14 \div 2 =$	**O.** $90 \div 10 =$

PART 2 Fractions, Decimals, and Percents

1. Find n to make each pair of fractions equivalent.

A. $\frac{4}{5} = \frac{n}{20}$	**B.** $\frac{9}{10} = \frac{36}{n}$	**C.** $\frac{4}{n} = \frac{28}{49}$
D. $\frac{n}{8} = \frac{4}{32}$	**E.** $\frac{5}{6} = \frac{n}{36}$	**F.** $\frac{3}{4} = \frac{60}{n}$

RATIO AND PROPORTION   DAB • Grade 5 • Unit 13 **201**

Discovery Assignment Book - page 201

*Answers for all the Home Practice in the *Discovery Assignment Book* are at the end of the unit.

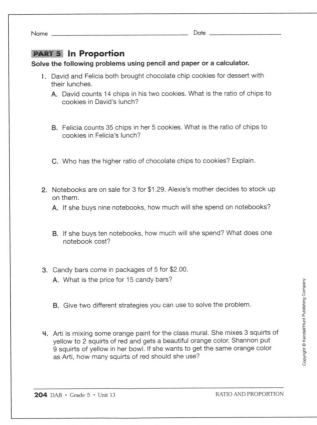

Discovery Assignment Book - page 202

Discovery Assignment Book (p. 202)

2. A. $\frac{1}{6} < 30\%$

B. $65\% > \frac{5}{8}$

C. $\frac{4}{9} < 46\%$

D. $0.66 < \frac{2}{3}$

E. $0.43 > \frac{3}{7}$

F. $\frac{6}{15} = 40\%$

Discovery Assignment Book - page 204

Discovery Assignment Book (p. 204)

Part 5. In Proportion

1. A. $\frac{14 \text{ chips}}{2 \text{ cookies}}$ or $\frac{7 \text{ chips}}{1 \text{ cookie}}$

B. $\frac{35 \text{ chips}}{5 \text{ cookies}}$ or $\frac{7 \text{ chips}}{1 \text{ cookie}}$

C. They both have the same ratio, since $\frac{14}{2}$ and $\frac{35}{5}$ both reduce to 7 chips per cookie.

2. A. $3.87

B. $4.30; $0.43

3. A. $6.00

B. $\frac{5}{\$2.00} = \frac{15}{C}$; $C = \$6.00$

Since 15 is 5×3, the price for 15 candy bars is $\$2.00 \times 3 = \$6.00$.

4. 6 squirts of red

Variables in Proportion

Lesson Overview

Estimated Class Sessions
2-3

Students investigate the concept of proportion as it applies to variables in an experiment. They reexamine variables they studied in the labs and activities this year and view them in the context of proportions. Students explore techniques for solving proportions.

Key Content

- Using ratios and proportions to solve problems.
- Using patterns in tables and graphs to make predictions and solve problems.
- Determining whether variables are in proportion.
- Expressing a multiplicative relationship between variables in proportion.
- Using numerical variables.
- Translating between different representations of ratios (graphical and symbolic).
- variables in proportion

Key Vocabulary

- variables in proportion

Homework

1. Assign the Homework section in the *Student Guide*.
2. Assign problems from Lesson 5.

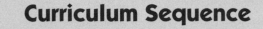

Curriculum Sequence

Before This Unit

Throughout third, fourth, and fifth grade, students completed experiments and activities in which they looked for the relationship between variables. Often, the variables are proportional to one another, and the resulting graph is a straight line through the origin (0, 0). Examples in fourth grade include the lab

Bouncing Ball in Unit 5 and *Downhill Racer* in Unit 10. In fifth grade, examples include the activity *Using Ratios* and the lab *Distance vs. Time* in Unit 3, the lab *Spreading Out* in Unit 4, and the lab *A Day at the Races* in Unit 5.

After This Unit

Students will investigate variables in proportion in the labs *Circumference vs. Diameter* in Unit 14 and *How Many Bats in a Cave?* in Unit 16.

Materials List

Supplies and Copies

Student	Teacher
Supplies for Each Student • calculator	**Supplies** • large graph paper, optional
Copies • 2 copies of *Centimeter Graph Paper* per student (*Unit Resource Guide* Page 34)	**Copies/Transparencies** • 4 transparencies of *Centimeter Graph Paper,* optional (*Unit Resource Guide* Page 34)

All blackline masters including assessment, transparency, and DPP masters are also on the Teacher Resource CD.

Student Books

Variables in Proportion (*Student Guide* Pages 402–410)

Beginning in third grade, students have studied the relationship between variables in their experiments and made predictions based on their observations. Many experiments involved variables that are in proportion. This activity gives students the opportunity to look more carefully at these experiments and to summarize some of the important properties of variables in proportion. See this unit's Background for a discussion of the properties of variables in proportion.

Part 1 *Distance vs. Time*

Ask students to turn to the *Variables in Proportion* Activity Pages in the *Student Guide*. Here, the concept of **variables in proportion** is illustrated with an example from the *Distance vs. Time* lab (from Unit 3). Two variables in an experiment are in proportion when their ratio is always the same. Read this example together; we will refer back to it as new ideas are introduced in the lesson. The data table is shown in Figure 4.

Distance vs. Time

Time in Seconds	Distance in Yards	$\dfrac{D}{t}$ Ratio in yd/sec
2	3	$\dfrac{3 \text{ yd}}{2 \text{ sec}}$
4	6	$\dfrac{6 \text{ yd}}{4 \text{ sec}}$
6	9	$\dfrac{9 \text{ yd}}{6 \text{ sec}}$

Figure 4: *Data table for* Distance vs. Time

Use *Questions 1–5* to lead a class discussion about the variables in the data table or have students answer them in small groups. *Question 1* asks students how they know that all the ratios in the table are equal to one another. One way to verify they are equal is to reduce them to lowest terms. Each ratio in the table is equivalent to $\frac{3 \text{ yd}}{2 \text{ sec}}$.

Students graph the data in *Question 2A* and describe the graph in *Question 2B*. Figure 5 shows a sample graph. Students should note that the graph is a straight line that goes uphill. The line meets the vertical axis at (0 s, 0 yd). *Question 3* asks students to choose two points on the line and write ratios corresponding to these points. Remind students that they did this when they did the *Distance vs. Time* lab in Unit 3.

Variables in Proportion

When scientists do experiments, they compare variables. They look for simple patterns that will help them better understand the variables and the way they are related. One especially useful pattern is the relationship of proportion. If the ratio of two variables in an experiment is always the same (or equivalent), the **variables are in proportion.**

For example, in the lab *Distance vs. Time* in Unit 3, we investigated the variables distance and time. A student walked at a steady pace. Other members of the group measured the time it took the student to travel different distances.

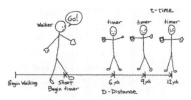

If you walk at a steady pace, then the ratio $\frac{distance}{time}$ is always the same. For example, if a student walks 3 yards every 2 seconds, then this data table shows the distance traveled (D) for several different times (t):

Distance vs. Time

Time in Seconds	Distance in Yards	$\dfrac{D}{t}$ Ratio in yd/sec
2	3	$\dfrac{3 \text{ yd}}{2 \text{ sec}}$
4	6	$\dfrac{6 \text{ yd}}{4 \text{ sec}}$
6	9	$\dfrac{9 \text{ yd}}{6 \text{ sec}}$

Student Guide - page 402

The ratio D/t is called the speed. It is usually written as a unit ratio. In the example, the student is walking at a speed of $\frac{1.5 \text{ yd}}{1 \text{ s}}$. We also write this as 1.5 yd/sec and say "1.5 yards per second."

Since the student walks at the same speed, the ratios in the table are all equal to one another.

Since the ratio D/t is always the same (even though D and t can be different), the variables distance and time are in proportion. We can write proportions using the ratios in the table. For example, $\frac{D}{t} = \frac{3 \text{ yd}}{2 \text{ sec}} = \frac{6 \text{ yd}}{4 \text{ sec}}$.

Discuss

Answer the following questions about the variables in the lab *Distance vs. Time* if the ratio of distance to time is 3 yards to 2 seconds.

1. Show how you know that all the ratios in the table are equal to one another.

2. A. Graph the variables in the data table. Write time (t) on the horizontal axis and distance (D) on the vertical axis.
   B. Describe your graph. Tell where it meets the vertical axis. Is it a straight line or a curve? Does it go up or down as you read from left to right?

3. Choose two points from your graph that lie on grid lines. Write the ratio of distance to time for each point. Are the two ratios equal?

4. A. If you double the time (t), what happens to the distance (D)? Give an example.
   B. If you triple the time (t), what happens to the distance (D)? Give an example.
   C. If you multiply the time by any number, what happens to the distance traveled? For example, if a student walks 3 yards in 2 seconds, how far will the student walk in 8 sec (4 × 2 sec)?

5. If you know the time, how can you find the distance? (*Hint:* How far does the walker travel on average in 1 second?)

Student Guide - page 403 (Answers on p. 50)

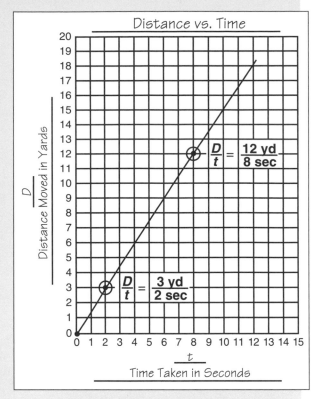

Figure 5: *Graph for Distance vs. Time*

Two points are circled on the line in Figure 5 and the ratios corresponding to these points are shown. These two ratios are equal: $\frac{3 \text{ yd}}{2 \text{ sec}} = \frac{12 \text{ yd}}{8 \text{ sec}}$.

Questions 4–5 explore the relationship between variables in proportion. If you double or triple one variable in proportion, the other variable will double or triple as well *(Questions 4A–4B)*. Using examples from *Distance vs. Time,* if a student walks 3 yards every 2 seconds, then he or she will walk 6 yards in 4 seconds and 9 yards in 6 seconds. In fact, if you multiply one variable by any number, the other variable will be increased by the same factor *(Question 4C)*. This is shown using equivalent fractions:

$$\frac{3 \text{ yd}}{2 \text{ sec}} = \frac{3 \text{ yd} \times 4}{2 \text{ sec} \times 4} = \frac{12 \text{ yd}}{8 \text{ sec}}$$

Question 5 asks students how they can find the distance traveled if they know how long the student walked. One way to answer this question is to find out how far the walker travels (on average) in 1 second. Dividing 3 yards by 2 seconds, students can see that the walker averages 1.5 yards in 1 second. We can write this as a unit ratio: $\frac{1.5 \text{ yd}}{1 \text{ sec}}$. Writing the ratio as a unit ratio can be very helpful when solving problems. Since we know how far the walker travels in one second, we can multiply to find out the distance traveled in any number of seconds. For example, the walker will travel 60×1.5 or 90 yards in 60 seconds.

Alternatively, encourage students to look for patterns in the data table moving across the rows, especially patterns using multiplication. In this case, the distance in yards is always $1\frac{1}{2}$ times the time ($D = 1\frac{1}{2} \times t$). For example, if the student walks for 6 seconds, the distance is $1\frac{1}{2}$ times 6, or 9 yards. We can apply this idea to larger numbers. If a student walks 20 seconds, he or she will walk $1\frac{1}{2} \times 20$, or 30 yards.

Part 2 Student Groups

Read together the examples of variables in proportion that students worked with in class this year. In groups, students **choose one** of the four examples listed and explore the proportional relationship between the variables involved. (Assign the examples to the groups to make sure each example is chosen.) Students work in groups to answer *Questions 6–10* using their examples. Groups will then share their results with the class.

Questions 6–10 are similar to *Questions 1–5.* Students complete a data table, draw a graph, and write a proportion that is true for the variables. Completed tables are shown in Figure 6 and completed graphs are shown in Figure 7.

TIMS Tip

Be sure students write the ratio as given, with the variable from the first column in the denominator and that from the second column in the numerator, and not the other way around. This order is used so when the data are graphed, in keeping with the convention that the first column variable goes on the horizontal axis, then this ratio corresponds to the steepness or slope of the line. The steeper the line, the greater the ratio. This will be useful in situations where we want to compare ratios, for instance, in the *Mass vs. Volume: Proportions and Density* lab in Lesson 4.

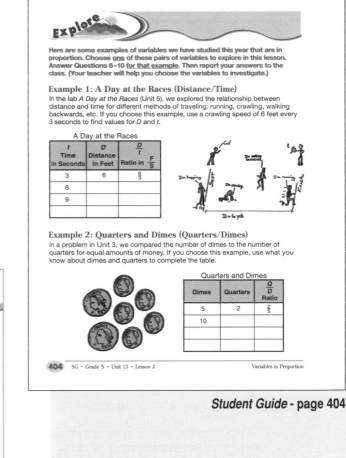

Explore

Here are some examples of variables we have studied this year that are in proportion. Choose <u>one</u> of these pairs of variables to explore in this lesson. Answer Questions 6–10 <u>for that example</u>. Then report your answers to the class. (Your teacher will help you choose the variables to investigate.)

Example 1: A Day at the Races (Distance/Time)
In the lab *A Day at the Races* (Unit 5), we explored the relationship between distance and time for different methods of traveling: running, crawling, walking backwards, etc. If you choose this example, use a crawling speed of 6 feet every 3 seconds to find values for *D* and *t*.

A Day at the Races

t Time in Seconds	D Distance in Feet	$\frac{D}{t}$ Ratio in $\frac{F}{S}$
3	6	$\frac{6}{3}$
6		
9		

Example 2: Quarters and Dimes (Quarters/Dimes)
In a problem in Unit 3, we compared the number of dimes to the number of quarters for equal amounts of money. If you choose this example, use what you know about dimes and quarters to complete the table.

Quarters and Dimes

Dimes	Quarters	$\frac{Q}{D}$ Ratio
5	2	$\frac{2}{5}$
10		

Student Guide - page 404

Example 3: Spreading Out (Area/Number of Drops)
In the lab *Spreading Out* (Unit 4), we made spots on paper towels by dropping different numbers of drops on a towel. Then we measured the area of the spots. As the number of drops increased, the area of the spots got larger. Alexis found that the ratio of the Area of the Spot to the Number of Drops was $\frac{11 \text{ sq cm}}{2 \text{ drops}}$. Use Alexis's ratio to complete the table.

Spreading Out

N Number of Drops	A Area in cm	$\frac{A}{N}$ Ratio
2	11	$\frac{11}{2}$
4		
6		

Example 4: Peanut Brittle (Peanuts/Sugar)
In Lesson 1 of this unit, we investigated a recipe for peanut brittle in which the ratio of the amount of peanuts to the amount of sugar was 1 c : 3 c. If you choose this example, use this ratio to complete the table.

Peanut Brittle

S Sugar (in cups)	P Peanuts (in cups)	$\frac{P}{S}$ Ratio
3	1	$\frac{1}{3}$
6		
9		

Answer Questions 6–10 for <u>one</u> of the four examples.

6. **A.** Complete the data table for your variables. Show at least 3 different values of your variables.
   B. Are the ratios in your table equal to one another? If so, tell how you know.

7. **A.** Graph the variables in the data table. Write the variable in the first column on the horizontal axis and the variable in the second column on the vertical axis. Choose the scale on each axis before you plot the points.
   B. Describe your graph. Tell where it meets the vertical axis. Is it a straight line or a curve? Does it go up or down as you read from left to right?

Student Guide - page 405 (Answers on p. 50)

A Day at the Races (crawling)

Example 1

t Time in Seconds	D Distance in Feet	$\dfrac{D}{t}$ Ratio in $\dfrac{F}{S}$
3	6	$\dfrac{6}{3}$
6	12	$\dfrac{12}{6}$
9	18	$\dfrac{18}{9}$

Quarters and Dimes

Example 2

Dimes	Quarters	$\dfrac{Q}{D}$ Ratio
5	2	$\dfrac{2}{5}$
10	4	$\dfrac{4}{10}$
15	6	$\dfrac{6}{15}$

Spreading Out

Example 3

N Number of Drops	A Area in sq cm	$\dfrac{A}{N}$ Ratio in $\dfrac{sq\ cm}{drop}$
2	11	$\dfrac{11}{2}$
4	22	$\dfrac{22}{4}$
6	33	$\dfrac{33}{6}$

Peanut Brittle

Example 4

S Sugar (in cups)	P Peanuts (in cups)	$\dfrac{P}{S}$ Ratio
3	1	$\dfrac{1}{3}$
6	2	$\dfrac{2}{6}$
9	3	$\dfrac{3}{9}$

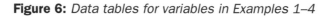

Figure 6: *Data tables for variables in Examples 1–4*

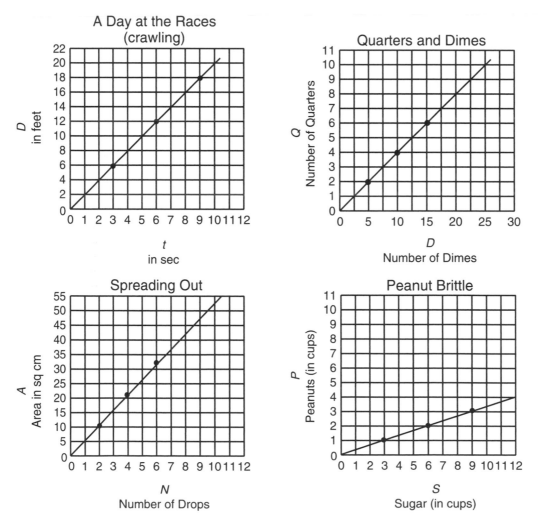

Figure 7: *Graphs for variables in Examples 1–4*

In *Questions 6–10,* students explore some of the properties of variables in proportion. After they answer the questions, have each group report their results to the class. By discovering the common results for different pairs of variables in proportion, students will be able to generalize what they learned and apply this knowledge to solve other problems. Use the following discussion prompts to help guide class discussion.

- *How can you show that all the ratios in your table are equal to one another (Question 6B)?* (One way is to reduce all the fractions to lowest terms.)

- *How are the graphs alike (Question 7)?* (All the graphs are straight lines that go through the point (0, 0). All the graphs go up as you read from left to right.)

- *If you double or triple the value of one variable, what happens to the other variable (Questions 9A–9B)?* (For all pairs of variables that are in proportion, doubling or tripling one variable will double or triple the other. For instance, in Example 4 if you double the number of cups of peanuts in the peanut brittle recipe, you must also double the number of cups of sugar.)

- *If you multiply one of your variables by any number, what happens to the other variable (Question 9C)?* (If you multiply one variable by a number, the other variable increases by the same factor. So if you are making a very large batch of peanut brittle in which the ratio of peanuts to sugar is $\frac{1}{3}$, then if you use 10 cups of peanuts, you must use 10 × 3 or 30 cups of sugar.)

- *How can you find one variable if you know the value of the other variable (Question 10)?* (Variables in proportion are always related by multiplication. Students can often see this if they look for patterns across the rows in the data tables. For instance, in Example 1 students can find the distance by multiplying the time by 2: $D = 2 \times t$. That is, if a student crawls for 9 seconds, we know that he or she will travel 2 × 9 or 18 yards. In Example 2, we can find the number of dimes equal in value to any number of quarters, by multiplying the number of quarters by $2\frac{1}{2}$: $D = 2\frac{1}{2} \times Q$. The value of 10 quarters is the same as the value of $2\frac{1}{2} \times 10$ or 25 dimes.) Often, finding the unit ratio is helpful. In Example 3, the ratio of area to number of drops in the *Spreading Out* experiment is 11 sq cm to 2 drops. Dividing 11 by 2, we can write the ratio as $\frac{5.5 \text{ sq cm}}{1 \text{ drop}}$. Knowing the area covered by 1 drop allows us to find the area for any number of drops.

TIMS Tip

Have groups share their graphs with the class by making them on transparencies of *Centimeter Graph Paper* or large graph paper.

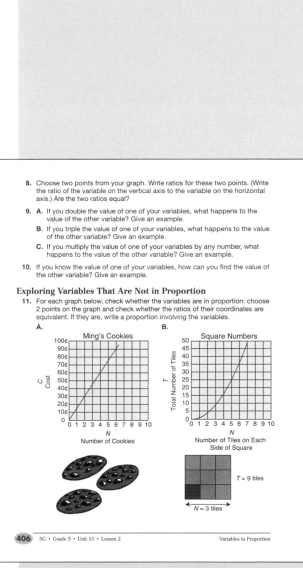

8. Choose two points from your graph. Write ratios for these two points. (Write the ratio of the variable on the vertical axis to the variable on the horizontal axis.) Are the two ratios equal?

9. A. If you double the value of one of your variables, what happens to the value of the other variable? Give an example.

   B. If you triple the value of one of your variables, what happens to the value of the other variable? Give an example.

   C. If you multiply the value of one of your variables by any number, what happens to the value of the other variable? Give an example.

10. If you know the value of one of your variables, how can you find the value of the other variable? Give an example.

Exploring Variables That Are Not in Proportion

11. For each graph below, check whether the variables are in proportion: choose 2 points on the graph and check whether the ratios of their coordinates are equivalent. If they are, write a proportion involving the variables.

406 SG • Grade 5 • Unit 13 • Lesson 2   Variables in Proportion

Student Guide - page 406 *(Answers on p. 51)*

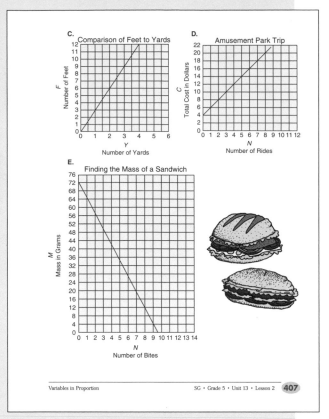

C.
Comparison of Feet to Yards

F
Number of Feet

Y
Number of Yards

D.
Amusement Park Trip

C
Total Cost in Dollars

N
Number of Rides

E.
Finding the Mass of a Sandwich

M
Mass in Grams

N
Number of Bites

Student Guide - page 407 (Answers on p. 51)

Part 3 **Exploring Variables That Are Not in Proportion**

Not all variables in experiments are in proportion. Those that are have the useful properties outlined in *Questions 6–10.* What about variables that are not in proportion? In *Question 11,* students examine graphs of several variables. Ask:

- *Are the graphs familiar? Tell the story of each graph.*

   Graphs A and C are from Unit 3 Lesson 5 *Using Ratios.* Graph A shows that as the number of cookies increases, the cost of the cookies increases as well. Graph C can be used as a tool for changing feet to yards and yards to feet.

   Graph B is from Unit 11 Lesson 3 *Patterns with Square Numbers.* In this lesson, students graphed the number of tiles along the side of a square and the number of tiles in the whole square. The resulting graph is the curve in Graph B.

   Graph D shows the total cost of going to an amusement park if the cost of admission into the park is $4 and each ride costs $2.

   Graph E is from a fourth grade experiment. Students find the mass of a sandwich. Then, they take bites out of the sandwich and find the mass of the remaining sandwich. The mass of the sandwich decreases as students take bites.

Students use the graphs to find out if the variables are in proportion. The variables in Graphs A and C are in proportion. However, the variables in Graphs B, D, and E are not. If the variables are in proportion, we can choose two points from the graph, write ratios corresponding to these two points, and see that the two ratios are equal. For example, to find out if the variables in Graph A are proportional, consider the points (2 cookies, 30¢) and (4 cookies, 60¢). The ratios $\frac{30 ¢}{2 \text{ cookies}}$ and $\frac{60 ¢}{4 \text{ cookies}}$ are equivalent fractions. In fact, any other point on the line would have a ratio equivalent to $\frac{15 ¢}{1 \text{ cookie}}$. (Students can choose other points until they are convinced of this.) Therefore, the variables number of cookies *(N)* and cost *(C)* are in proportion and a proportion between them is expressed by $\frac{N}{C} = \frac{15 ¢}{1 \text{ cookie}}$.

The variables in Graph B are not in proportion. Consider the points (4, 16) and (5, 25) or any other pair of points on the graph. The ratios $\frac{16}{4}$ and $\frac{25}{5}$ are not equivalent. Therefore, the variables on this graph are not in proportion. Similar comparisons for the other graphs will help the students determine which graphs represent variables in proportion.

Rather than checking for a proportion, we can quickly tell whether or not variables are in proportion by examining their graphs. In **Question 12,** students should look back over their graphs to find what features are shared by graphs of variables in proportion. Graphs A and C, which represent variables in proportion, are both straight lines and they both include the origin (0, 0). In fact, any graph that is a straight line graph through (0, 0) represents variables in proportion and any graph that is not represents variables that are not in proportion.

Question 13 asks students to choose a graph from **Question 11** that represents variables that are not in proportion and examine the multiplication property they explored in **Question 9.** Let's choose Graph E, for example, and choose a value of $N = 4$ bites. Using the graph, we see that after 4 bites were taken from the sandwich, the mass of the sandwich was 42 grams ($M = 42$ grams). If we double the number of bites ($N = 8$ bites), then we see from the graph that the mass of the sandwich is only 12 grams ($M = 12$ grams). Obviously, doubling the number of bites did not double the mass of the sandwich. Therefore, the variables N and M are not in proportion.

Part 4 **Solving Problems Using Graphs of Variables in Proportion**

Graphs are useful because they display the relationship between the variables. When the variables are in proportion, the data points lie on a straight line, and we can use that line to make very good predictions. One of the beauties of nature is that many variables are related in this simple way. In **Questions 14–15,** students use graphs of variables in proportion to solve problems. The skills practiced here can be applied again in the lab *Mass vs. Volume* in Lesson 4 of this unit, in the labs in Units 14 and 16, and in any other situation where the graph is a straight line through (0, 0). This type of graph is very common; remind students, however, that the techniques will not work for other types of graphs.

Read the beginning of this section which describes John's bouncing ball problem. For students who did not do the experiment in fourth grade, illustrate it by dropping a ball from different heights. Students should see that the higher the drop height, *D,* the higher the bounce height, *B.* The relationship between *D* and *B* for John's tennis ball is shown on the graph. In **Question 14A** students solve the proportion:

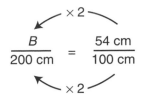

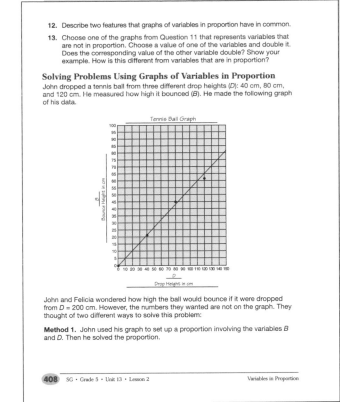

12. Describe two features that graphs of variables in proportion have in common.

13. Choose one of the graphs from Question 11 that represents variables that are not in proportion. Choose a value of one of the variables and double it. Does the corresponding value of the other variable double? Show your example. How is this different from variables that are in proportion?

Solving Problems Using Graphs of Variables in Proportion

John dropped a tennis ball from three different drop heights (*D*): 40 cm, 80 cm, and 120 cm. He measured how high it bounced (*B*). He made the following graph of his data.

John and Felicia wondered how high the ball would bounce if it were dropped from *D* = 200 cm. However, the numbers they wanted are not on the graph. They thought of two different ways to solve this problem:

Method 1. John used his graph to set up a proportion involving the variables *B* and *D*. Then he solved the proportion.

408 SG • Grade 5 • Unit 13 • Lesson 2　　　　　　　　　Variables in Proportion

Student Guide - page 408 (Answers on p. 52)

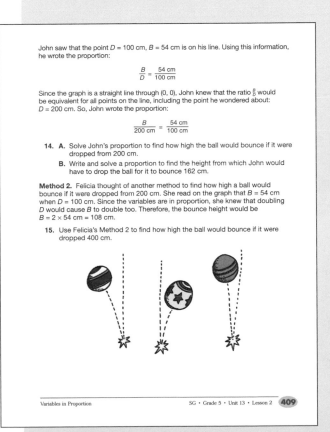

John saw that the point *D* = 100 cm, *B* = 54 cm is on his line. Using this information, he wrote the proportion:

$$\frac{B}{D} = \frac{54 \text{ cm}}{100 \text{ cm}}$$

Since the graph is a straight line through (0, 0), John knew that the ratio $\frac{B}{D}$ would be equivalent for all points on the line, including the point he wondered about: *D* = 200 cm. So, John wrote the proportion:

$$\frac{B}{200 \text{ cm}} = \frac{54 \text{ cm}}{100 \text{ cm}}$$

14. A. Solve John's proportion to find how high the ball would bounce if it were dropped from 200 cm.
    B. Write and solve a proportion to find the height from which John would have to drop the ball for it to bounce 162 cm.

Method 2. Felicia thought of another method to find how high a ball would bounce if it were dropped from 200 cm. She read on the graph that *B* = 54 cm when *D* = 100 cm. Since the variables are in proportion, she knew that doubling *D* would cause *B* to double too. Therefore, the bounce height would be *B* = 2 × 54 cm = 108 cm.

15. Use Felicia's Method 2 to find how high the ball would bounce if it were dropped from 400 cm.

Variables in Proportion　　　　　　　　　SG • Grade 5 • Unit 13 • Lesson 2　**409**

Student Guide - page 409 (Answers on p. 52)

$$\overset{\times 2}{\overbrace{}}$$
$$\frac{B}{200 \text{ cm}} = \frac{54 \text{ cm}}{100 \text{ cm}}$$
$$\underset{\times 2}{\underbrace{}}$$

The denominator on the left-hand side is twice the denominator on the right-hand side. Because the ratios are equivalent, the numerators should have the same relationship. Therefore, $B = 2 \times 54$ cm $= 108$ cm.

In **Question 14B,** students write and solve the proportion:

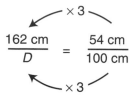

Here, the numerator on the left-hand side is three times that on the right-hand side, and because the ratios are equivalent, the denominators are related the same way. This means $D = 3 \times 100$ cm $= 300$ cm. If students do not observe that one numerator is three times the other, they can determine the factor relating the numerators by dividing: $162 \div 54 = 3$, so 162 is 3 times 54. The numbers in this example are, admittedly, contrived to come out nicely. But even in cases where the numbers are "messy," students can divide on their calculators or estimate to find the factor that relates the numerators or denominators.

In **Question 15,** students use a related method to find how high the ball would bounce if it were dropped 400 cm. $D = 400$ cm is not on the graph, but $D = 100$ cm is on the graph. A ball dropped from $D = 100$ cm bounces $B = 54$ cm. Therefore, a ball dropped from 4 times that height, $D = 400$ cm, would bounce 4 times that amount, $B = 4 \times 54$ cm $= 216$ cm. Remind students that this method works because D and B are in proportion, as they can see from the graph which is a straight line through $(0, 0)$. This method is an application of the fact they observed in **Question 9** that multiplying one variable results in the multiplication of the other by the same factor. As they observed in **Question 13,** this method does not work if the variables are not in proportion.

Homework and Practice

- Assign the Homework section in the *Student Guide* for additional practice.

- Assign problems from Lesson 5 *Problems of Scale* for homework.

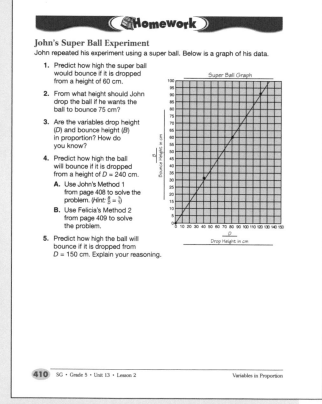

Student Guide - page 410 *(Answers on p. 53)*

At a Glance

Part 1. Distance vs. Time

1. Use the *Variables in Proportion* Activity Pages in the *Student Guide* to illustrate the concept of variables in proportion.
2. Discuss *Questions 1–5* about the variables in the *Distance vs. Time* data table.

Part 2. Student Groups

1. Read together the examples of variables in proportion on the *Variables in Proportion* Activity Pages in the *Student Guide.*
2. Assign one example to each group of students.
3. Students work in groups to answer *Questions 6–10* for their examples. They make data tables, draw a graph, and write proportions for the variables.

Part 3. Exploring Variables That Are Not in Proportion

1. Students explore variables not in proportion in the Exploring Variables That Are Not in Proportion section.
2. In *Questions 11–12,* students tell the stories of the graphs and determine which graphs display variables that are in proportion.
3. Students explore the multiplicative property of variables in proportion in *Question 13.*

Part 4. Solving Problems Using Graphs of Variables in Proportion

Students solve proportional reasoning problems using two methods in *Questions 14–15.*

Homework

1. Assign the Homework section in the *Student Guide.*
2. Assign problems from Lesson 5.

Answer Key is on pages 50–53.

Notes:

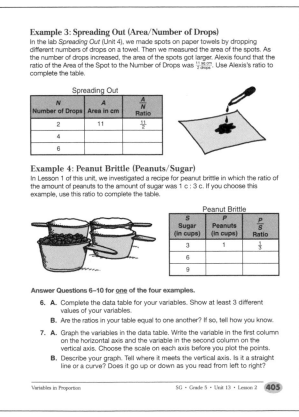

Student Guide - page 403

Student Guide (p. 403)

1. Since all the ratios in the table reduce to $\frac{3}{2}$, they are all equal.*

2. A. See Figure 5 in the Lesson Guide.*

   B. The graph is a straight line that goes up as we read from left to right and it meets the vertical axis at (0, 0).

3. Answers will vary. See Figure 5 in Lesson Guide 2 for two possible solutions.*

4. A. The distance also doubles. $\frac{3 \text{ yd}}{2 \text{ sec}} = \frac{6 \text{ yd}}{4 \text{ sec}}$ *

   B. The distance also triples. $\frac{3 \text{ yd}}{2 \text{ sec}} = \frac{9 \text{ yd}}{6 \text{ sec}}$

   C. If we multiply the time by any number, the distance will increase by the same factor.
   $\frac{3 \text{ yd}}{2 \text{ sec}} = \frac{3 \text{ yd} \times 4}{2 \text{ sec} \times 4} = \frac{12 \text{ yd}}{8 \text{ sec}}$

5. One way to find this answer is to find the distance traveled in one second and then multiply this by the number of seconds traveled.*

Student Guide - page 405

Student Guide (p. 405)

6.* A. See Figure 6 in Lesson Guide 2.

   B. The ratios are all the same since they all reduce to the same fraction.

7. A. See Figure 7 in Lesson Guide 2.*

   B. All the graphs are straight lines that go up as we read from left to right and they all meet the vertical axis at the point (0, 0).

*Answers and/or discussion are included in the Lesson Guide.

Student Guide (pp. 406–407)

8. Answers will vary. The ratios should be equal.

9.* **A.** For all pairs of variables that are in proportion, if we double the value of one variable, the value of the other variable will also double. In Example 1, if we double the distance, the time will also double.

B. For all pairs of variables that are in proportion, if we triple the value of one variable, the value of the other variable will also triple. In Example 1, if we triple the distance, the time will also triple.

C. For all pairs of variables that are in proportion, if we multiply one variable by any number, the value of the other variable increases by the same factor. In Example 4, since the ratio of peanuts to sugar is $\frac{1}{3}$, if we use 10 cups of peanuts, we must use $10 \times 3 = 30$ cups of sugar.

10. If we know the value of one of the variables, we can use patterns in the table to find the value of the other variable. In Example 1, we can find the distance by multiplying the time by 2. We can also set up a proportion such as $\frac{D}{T} = \frac{6}{3} = \frac{?}{9}$.*

11.* **A.** Choosing the points (2 cookies, 30¢) and (4 cookies, 60¢), the ratios $\frac{30¢}{2}$ and $\frac{60¢}{4}$ are equivalent fractions. Therefore, the variables N and C are in proportion.

B. Choosing the points (4, 16) and (5, 25), the ratios $\frac{16}{4}$ and $\frac{25}{5}$ are not equivalent fractions. Therefore, the variables N and T are not in proportion.

C. Choosing the points (2, 6) and (3, 9), the ratios $\frac{6}{2}$ and $\frac{9}{3}$ are equivalent fractions. Therefore, the variables Y and F are in proportion.

D. Choosing the points (2, 8) and (4, 12), the ratios $\frac{8}{2}$ and $\frac{12}{4}$ are not equivalent fractions. Therefore, the variables N and C are not in proportion.

E. Choosing the points (8, 12) and (9, 4), the ratios $\frac{12}{8}$ and $\frac{4}{9}$ are not equivalent fractions. Therefore, the variables N and M are not in proportion.

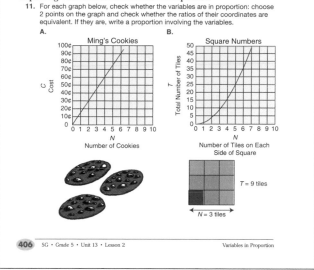

Student Guide - page 406

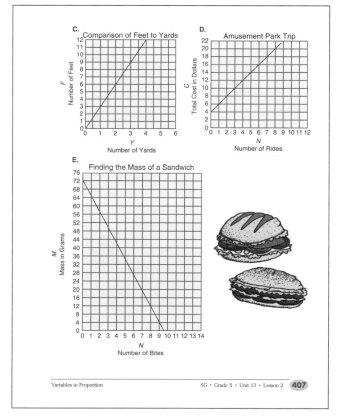

Student Guide - page 407

*Answers and/or discussion are included in the Lesson Guide.

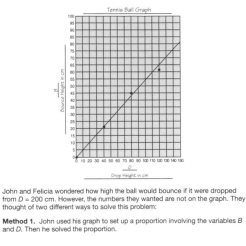

12. Describe two features that graphs of variables in proportion have in common.

13. Choose one of the graphs from Question 11 that represents variables that are not in proportion. Choose a value of one of the variables and double it. Does the corresponding value of the other variable double? Show your example. How is this different from variables that are in proportion?

Solving Problems Using Graphs of Variables in Proportion
John dropped a tennis ball from three different drop heights (*D*): 40 cm, 80 cm, and 120 cm. He measured how high it bounced (*B*). He made the following graph of his data.

John and Felicia wondered how high the ball would bounce if it were dropped from *D* = 200 cm. However, the numbers they wanted are not on the graph. They thought of two different ways to solve this problem:

Method 1. John used his graph to set up a proportion involving the variables *B* and *D*. Then he solved the proportion.

Student Guide - page 408

John saw that the point *D* = 100 cm, *B* = 54 cm is on his line. Using this information, he wrote the proportion:

$$\frac{B}{D} = \frac{54 \text{ cm}}{100 \text{ cm}}$$

Since the graph is a straight line through (0, 0), John knew that the ratio $\frac{B}{D}$ would be equivalent for all points on the line, including the point he wondered about: *D* = 200 cm. So, John wrote the proportion:

$$\frac{B}{200 \text{ cm}} = \frac{54 \text{ cm}}{100 \text{ cm}}$$

14. **A.** Solve John's proportion to find how high the ball would bounce if it were dropped from 200 cm.

   B. Write and solve a proportion to find the height from which John would have to drop the ball for it to bounce 162 cm.

Method 2. Felicia thought of another method to find how high a ball would bounce if it were dropped from 200 cm. She read on the graph that *B* = 54 cm when *D* = 100 cm. Since the variables are in proportion, she knew that doubling *D* would cause *B* to double too. Therefore, the bounce height would be *B* = 2 × 54 cm = 108 cm.

15. Use Felicia's Method 2 to find how high the ball would bounce if it were dropped 400 cm.

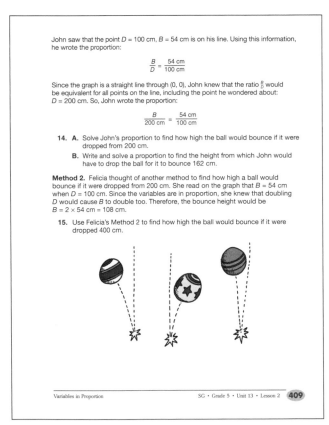

Student Guide - page 409

Student Guide (p. 408)

12. The graphs of variables in proportion are straight lines and they always meet the vertical axis at the point (0, 0).*

13. Using Graph D, for 2 rides the total cost is $8. If we double the number of rides to 4 rides, we can see from the graph that the total cost is only $12. Doubling the number of rides did not double the cost. Therefore, the variables *N* and *C* are not in proportion.*

Student Guide (p. 409)

14.* **A.** $B = 108$ cm
   B. $\frac{B}{D} = \frac{162 \text{ cm}}{?} = \frac{54 \text{ cm}}{100 \text{ cm}}$, $? = 300$ cm
15. $B = 4 \times 54$ cm $= 216$ cm*

*Answers and/or discussion are included in the Lesson Guide.

Student Guide (p. 410)

Homework

1. About 45 cm

2. 100 cm

3. Since the ratios $\frac{45}{60}$ and $\frac{75}{100}$ both reduce to the same fraction, $\frac{3}{4}$, the variables D and B are in proportion.

4. **A.** $\frac{B}{D} = \frac{?}{240 \text{ cm}} = \frac{45 \text{ cm}}{60 \text{ cm}}$; ? = 180 cm
   B. Since $240 = 60 \times 4$, $B = 45 \times 4 = 180$ cm.

5. $\frac{B}{D} = \frac{75 \text{ cm}}{100 \text{ cm}} = \frac{?}{150 \text{ cm}}$; ? $= 112\frac{1}{2}$ cm or since B is about 37 cm when D is 50 cm, the bounce height will be about 3×37 or about 111 cm for a drop height of 150 cm.

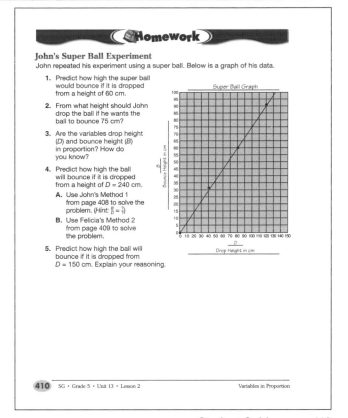

Student Guide - page 410

Lesson 3

Sink and Float

Lesson Overview

Estimated Class Sessions

3

Students investigate why things sink or float in water. They find the mass and volume of several objects and observe which objects sink and which float. They observe that sinking and floating are related to both mass and volume. Density is introduced as the ratio of mass to volume. The densities of the objects are computed, and a pattern is discovered that predicts whether an object will sink or float in water.

Key Content

- Using tables and fractions to express ratios.
- Measuring mass.
- Measuring volume by displacement.
- Defining density as a ratio.
- Using patterns in data tables to make predictions and solve problems.

- Connecting mathematics and science to real-world situations: investigating density.
- Connecting measurement, data analysis, and proportional reasoning.

Key Vocabulary

- density

Math Facts

Use DPP items E, H, and I to review division facts.

Homework

Assign Part 3 of the Home Practice.

Assessment

Use the *Observational Assessment Record* to note students' abilities to use ratios and proportions to solve problems.

Curriculum Sequence

Before This Unit

Students measured volume by displacement using graduated cylinders in Grades 2–4. They also measured mass using two-pan balances in Grades 2–4.

Students found the volume of prisms in Grade 4 Unit 9.

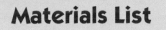

Materials List

Supplies and Copies

Student	Teacher
Supplies for Each Student Group	**Supplies**
• two-pan balance • set of gram masses • 250-cc graduated cylinder • 100-cc graduated cylinder • small piece of clay for leveling the balance • paper towels • water • eyedropper • cup or beaker for pouring water • large container (dishpan) of water • several small objects that sink or float (rock, marble, cork, clay, 1-inch diameter steel or plastic sphere, wood, paraffin block) • ruler to measure paraffin • calculator	
Copies	**Copies/Transparencies**
• 1 copy of *Mass Review* per student, optional (*Unit Resource Guide* Pages 64–65) • 1 copy of *Volume Review* per student, optional (*Unit Resource Guide* Pages 66–68)	

All blackline masters including assessment, transparency, and DPP masters are also on the Teacher Resource CD.

Student Books
Sink and Float (*Student Guide* Pages 411–414)
Sink and Float Tables (*Discovery Assignment Book* Page 205)

Daily Practice and Problems and Home Practice
DPP items E–J (*Unit Resource Guide* Pages 15–18)
Home Practice Part 3 (*Discovery Assignment Book* Page 202)

Note: Classrooms whose pacing differs significantly from the suggested pacing of the units should use the Math Facts Calendar in Section 4 of the *Facts Resource Guide* to ensure students receive the complete math facts program.

Assessment Tools
Observational Assessment Record (*Unit Resource Guide* Pages 11–12)

Suggestions for using the DPPs are on page 62.

E. Bit: Practicing the Facts (URG p. 15) ▢⁵ˣ⁷

A. $200 \div 40 =$ B. $640 \div 80 =$
C. $400 \div 10 =$ D. $1200 \div 60 =$
E. $900 \div 90 =$ F. $490 \div 70 =$
G. $8000 \div 40 =$ H. $40{,}000 \div 80 =$
I. $1800 \div 20 =$ J. $400 \div 20 =$

F. Task: Speaking of Parts (URG p. 16) [N]

Remember that fractions, decimals, and percents
are all ways of speaking about parts of a whole.
Fill in the chart with equivalent names for the given
numbers. Reduce all fractions to lowest terms.

	Fraction	Decimal	Percent
A.		0.10	
B.	$\frac{1}{2}$		
C.			15%
D.		0.4	
E.	$\frac{3}{100}$		
F.			30%
G.	$\frac{3}{4}$		
H.		0.01	

G. Bit: Line Segments (URG p. 16) [⚖] [N]

The ratio of the lengths of two line segments is 2:3.

A. If the first line segment is 4 cm long, then what is
   the length of the second segment? Draw both line
   segments. Write the length on each segment.
B. If the second segment is 12 cm long, then what is
   the length of the first segment? Draw both line
   segments. Write the length on each segment.

H. Task: Remainders (URG p. 17) [N] ▢⁵ˣ⁷ ✖

Solve the following problems. Write the quotients
first as whole numbers with remainders, then as
mixed numbers, and finally as decimals.

A. $42 \div 5 =$

B. $19 \div 5 =$

C. $7 \div 5 =$

I. Bit: More Facts (URG p. 17) ▢⁵ˣ⁷

Find the value of n that makes these number
sentences true.

A. $80 \div 10 = n$ B. $n \div 8 = 2$
C. $30 \div n = 5$ D. $16 \div n = 4$
E. $n \div 9 = 5$ F. $100 \div 10 = n$
G. $100 \div 5 = n$ H. $n \div 3 = 10$
I. $60 \div 2 = n$ J. $9 \div n = 3$

J. Task: Founding Fathers Who Became Presidents (URG p. 18) 🕐 ✖

Founding Father	Birth	Death	President
George Washington	1732	1799	1789–1797
John Adams	1735	1826	1797–1801
Thomas Jefferson	1743	1826	1801–1809
James Madison	1751	1836	1809–1817

A. Which president lived the longest?
B. Who was the youngest of the four
   presidents when he took office?
C. Which presidents served two terms?
D. How old was Thomas Jefferson when
   James Madison became president?
E. Madison became president _____ years
   after Washington's death.

Before the Activity

If you need to make substitutions as you gather materials, be sure to include objects that will reveal some of the misconceptions students might have about why things sink and float. Some children think things sink only "because they are big" or "because they are heavy." You will need an object that is big compared to the others but does not sink, such as a block of paraffin or a piece of plastic foam. You will also need an object that is heavy compared to the others but does not sink. The paraffin block serves both of these purposes. A bar of soap that floats also works well.

TIMS Tip

Paraffin blocks should be available at a supermarket (in the canning section) or at a craft store. Pieces of wood or wax candles will float and can also be substituted for the paraffin block as long as they are larger and heavier than some of the items that sink.

If students need to review the techniques for finding mass and volume, use the *Mass Review* and *Volume Review* Activity Pages in the *Unit Resource Guide.* These activities are taken from lessons in Grades 3 and 4. You may also wish to refer to the TIMS Tutors: *The Concept of Mass* and *The Concept of Volume* in the *Teacher Implementation Guide.*

Teaching the Activity

Part 1 Introduction

Read together the vignette on the *Sink and Float* Activity Pages in the *Student Guide.* In it, Luis points out that ships are both big and heavy and asks, "Why do they float?" Discuss:

• *What properties determine whether objects sink or float?*

Some students might suggest sinking has something to do with how heavy the object is (its mass or weight). Others might suggest it has something to do with how big the object is (its volume). Tell students they will explore both mass and volume and see whether they can find a pattern to help predict whether things will sink (or float).

Part 2 Collecting Mass and Volume Data

In *Questions 1–4,* students measure the mass of several objects and observe that mass alone does not determine whether an object will sink or float. In *Questions 5–7,* they measure the volume of the same objects and observe that volume alone does not determine whether an object will sink or float.

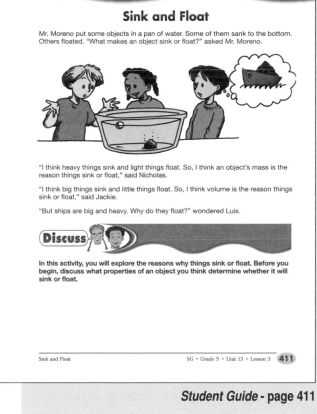

Sink and Float

Mr. Moreno put some objects in a pan of water. Some of them sank to the bottom. Others floated. "What makes an object sink or float?" asked Mr. Moreno.

"I think heavy things sink and light things float. So, I think an object's mass is the reason things sink or float," said Nicholas.

"I think big things sink and little things float. So, I think volume is the reason things sink or float," said Jackie.

"But ships are big and heavy. Why do they float?" wondered Luis.

Discuss

In this activity, you will explore the reasons why things sink or float. Before you begin, discuss what properties of an object you think determine whether it will sink or float.

Sink and Float   SG • Grade 5 • Unit 13 • Lesson 3   **411**

Student Guide - page 411

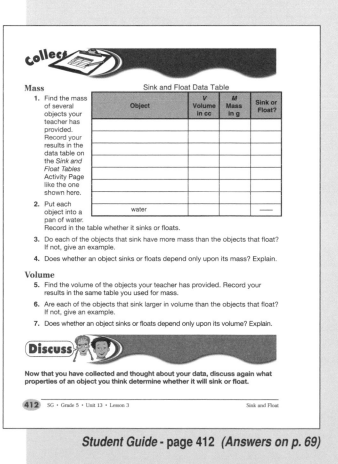

Mass

Sink and Float Data Table

1. Find the mass of several objects your teacher has provided. Record your results in the data table on the *Sink and Float Tables* Activity Page like the one shown here.

Object	V Volume in cc	M Mass in g	Sink or Float?
water			—

2. Put each object into a pan of water. Record in the table whether it sinks or floats.

3. Do each of the objects that sink have more mass than the objects that float? If not, give an example.

4. Does whether an object sinks or floats depend only upon its mass? Explain.

Volume

5. Find the volume of the objects your teacher has provided. Record your results in the same table you used for mass.

6. Are each of the objects that sink larger in volume than the objects that float? If not, give an example.

7. Does whether an object sinks or floats depend only upon its volume? Explain.

Discuss

Now that you have collected and thought about your data, discuss again what properties of an object you think determine whether it will sink or float.

412   SG • Grade 5 • Unit 13 • Lesson 3   Sink and Float

Student Guide - page 412 (Answers on p. 69)

Sink and Float Tables

Sink and Float Data Table

Object	V Volume in cc	M Mass in g	Sink or Float?
water			—

Density of water as a ratio: _____

Density of water as a decimal: _____

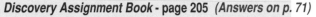

	Sinks in Water				Floats in Water		
Object	Density as Ratio $\frac{M}{V}$	Density as Decimal		Object	Density as Ratio $\frac{M}{V}$	Density as Decimal	

Sink and Float   DAB • Grade 5 • Unit 13 • Lesson 3 **205**

Discovery Assignment Book - page 205 *(Answers on p. 71)*

Students record their data on the *Sink and Float Tables* Activity Page in the *Discovery Assignment Book.* Sample data are displayed in Figure 8.

The paraffin block won't fit in the graduated cylinder, so we need to measure its volume another way. One way is to measure the dimensions of the block and then compute its volume on a calculator by multiplying length × width × height. The block used in our sample had dimensions:

$$12.6 \text{ cm} \times 6.2 \text{ cm} \times 1.4 \text{ cm}$$

and a volume of approximately 109 cc. Children should measure the block's length, width, and height to the nearest tenth of a centimeter. Because of irregularities in the block and the fact that we are multiplying approximations (in length, width, and height), the final result for the block's volume may not be very accurate.

Sink and Float Data Table

Object	V Volume in cc	M Mass in g	Sink or Float?
rock	8.3 cc	24 g	S
cork	13.0 cc	2 g	F
clay	14.1 cc	29 g	S
steel sphere (1 inch diameter)	8.5 cc	63 g	S
plastic sphere (1 inch diameter)	8.5 cc	10 g	S
wood	16.0 cc	7 g	F
paraffin	109 cc	90 g	F
water	50 cc	49 g	—

Figure 8: *Sample data*

By collecting data, students will observe that sinking and floating do not depend only on mass or only on volume. At this point, ask students again what properties they think determine whether an object will sink or float. In the discussion, they might suggest that sinking and floating have something to do with both mass and volume. In the next section, they will refine this idea and learn about density.

TIMS Tip

Use DPP Task F to review translating between fractions, decimals, and percents. Students will use these skills in Part 3 of this lesson.

Part 3 Density

Sinking and floating depend not on mass or volume alone but on the ratio of mass to volume. This ratio is called **density.** Students write the densities of the objects in their tables in *Question 8.* To help them find a pattern, they organize their density information in a table of objects that sink and a separate table of objects that float. It is often easier to compare densities if they are expressed as unit ratios. After expressing density as the ratio $\frac{mass}{volume}$, students can divide on their calculators to find the unit ratio, as shown in the table in Figure 9.

Sinks in Water

Object	Density as Ratio $\frac{M}{V}$	Density as Decimal
rock	$\frac{24\text{ g}}{8.3\text{ cc}}$	$\frac{2.9\text{ g}}{1\text{ cc}}$
piece of clay	$\frac{29\text{ g}}{14.1\text{ cc}}$	$\frac{2.1\text{ g}}{1\text{ cc}}$
steel sphere	$\frac{63\text{ g}}{8.5\text{ cc}}$	$\frac{7.4\text{ g}}{1\text{ cc}}$
plastic sphere	$\frac{10\text{ g}}{8.5\text{ cc}}$	$\frac{1.2\text{ g}}{1\text{ cc}}$

Floats in Water

Object	Density as Ratio $\frac{M}{V}$	Density as Decimal
piece of cork	$\frac{2\text{ g}}{13\text{ cc}}$	$\frac{0.2\text{ g}}{1\text{ cc}}$
piece of wood	$\frac{7\text{ g}}{16\text{ cc}}$	$\frac{0.4\text{ g}}{1\text{ cc}}$
paraffin block	$\frac{90\text{ g}}{109\text{ cc}}$	$\frac{0.8\text{ g}}{1\text{ cc}}$

Density of water as a decimal: $\frac{1.0\text{ g}}{1\text{ cc}}$

Figure 9: *Densities of objects that sink and objects that float*

Scientists usually write an object's density as a number followed by the units g/cc (pronounced grams per cc). For example, the density of steel is 7.4 g/cc. We will usually write the density of steel as $\frac{7.4\text{ g}}{1\text{ cc}}$ to emphasize that density is a ratio.

Student Guide - page 413 (Answers on p. 69)

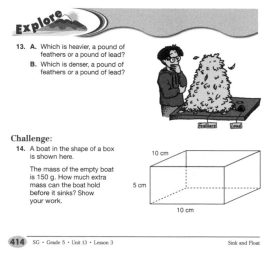

9. **A.** Find the mass and the volume of an easy to measure amount of water. (*Hint:* Be sure to subtract the mass of the cylinder.) Record your data in the Sink and Float Data Table.

   B. What is the density of the water? Write your answer as a ratio and as a decimal in the space provided on the *Sink and Float Tables* Activity Page. Is it greater than one, less than one, close to one, or equal to one?

Finding Patterns

10. Look at your tables. What patterns do you see about objects that sink and those that float in water? Write your conclusions in sentences.

11. An object has a mass of 30 g and a volume of 40 cc. Will it sink or float in water?

12. Will an object with a mass of 500 g sink or float in water?

Explore

13. **A.** Which is heavier, a pound of feathers or a pound of lead?

    B. Which is denser, a pound of feathers or a pound of lead?

Challenge:

14. A boat in the shape of a box is shown here.

    The mass of the empty boat is 150 g. How much extra mass can the boat hold before it sinks? Show your work.

    10 cm

    5 cm

    10 cm

Student Guide - page 414 (Answers on p. 70)

In *Question 9,* students find the mass, volume, and density of water. They first measure the mass of the empty graduated cylinder. They then pour an easy-to-measure amount of water into the cylinder, say 50 cc of water, and record its volume. An eye-dropper is useful for putting in the last few drops. Next, they find the total mass of the water and the cylinder combined. To compute the mass of the water alone, they need to subtract the mass of the cylinder from the total mass.

> ## Content Note
>
> **Density of Water.** When the metric system was developed, the gram was defined to be the mass of 1 cubic centimeter of water (at standard temperature and air pressure). So, by definition, the density of water is 1 gram per cubic centimeter, or 1 g/cc.

In our sample data, the mass of the water was 49 g and the volume was 50 cc. Thus, the density was $\frac{49\,\text{g}}{50\,\text{cc}}$. This is close to one. The density of water is $\frac{1\,\text{g}}{1\,\text{cc}}$, but because of the limitation of your measuring equipment and impurities in the water, you should not be disappointed if your results are not exactly $\frac{1\,\text{g}}{1\,\text{cc}}$. We computed 49 g ÷ 50 cc = $\frac{0.98}{1\,\text{cc}}$. We rounded this to the nearest tenth and recorded $\frac{1.0\,\text{g}}{1\,\text{cc}}$ in the table.

Part 4 Finding Patterns

After computing densities, students look for patterns in their tables to help them predict whether an object will sink or float in water *(Question 10).* These are some of the patterns they might notice:

- If the mass of an object (in grams) is larger than its volume (in cubic centimeters), then it sinks; otherwise it floats.

- If the density of an object is greater than 1 g/cc (the density of water), then it sinks; otherwise it floats.

Students apply their pattern in *Question 11.* They determine that the density of the object is $\frac{M}{V} = \frac{30\,\text{g}}{40\,\text{cc}} = \frac{.75\,\text{g}}{1\,\text{cc}}$, which is less than 1 g/cc. Therefore, the object will float. To answer *Question 12,* they should reply that there isn't enough information to determine whether the object will sink or float. We need to know its volume as well as its mass.

Part 5 **Tying It Together**

Question 13A is an old riddle: Which is heavier, a pound of feathers or a pound of lead? This is a trick question, but if children aren't fooled, they will say, "neither, they both weigh the same amount— 1 pound." *Question 13B* is not a trick: Which is denser, a pound of feathers or a pound of lead? To compare the densities, we only have to look at the volumes, since the masses are the same. The volume of a pound of lead is much smaller than the volume of a pound of feathers, so the denominator in the density $\frac{M}{V}$ is smaller for lead than feathers. Since the numerators are the same, the density of lead is greater than the density of feathers.

Some students might enjoy solving the Challenge *Question 14.* The mass of the empty boat is $M = 150$ g. Its volume is 10 cm $\times$ 10 cm $\times$ 5 cm = 500 cc. The density of the empty boat is $\frac{150\text{ g}}{500\text{ cc}}$, so, of course, the empty boat will float. The numerator is less than the denominator (in other words, the ratio is less than 1 g/cc). Putting cargo in the boat will increase the mass (the numerator), but not the volume. As long as the extra mass is less than 350 g, the total mass will be less than 500 g. Then, the ratio $\frac{M}{V}$ will be less than $\frac{500\text{ g}}{500\text{ cc}} = 1$ g/cc, and the boat will float.

In this lesson, students found that objects will float in water if their densities are less than the density of water (1 g/cc). In the next lesson, they will explore the density of different substances. They will see that the density of a substance, such as steel or paraffin, is the same no matter the size of a sample. In other words, the mass of a substance is proportional to the volume. They will also investigate the relation between the mass and the volume of a substance using data from this activity.

TIMS Tip

Students should save their data for use in the next lesson.

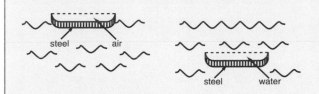

2. For each pair of numbers write a number sentence using <, >, and =.
   (*Hint:* Use a calculator to change the fractions to decimals.)

   A. $\frac{1}{6}$ and 30%　　　B. 65% and $\frac{5}{8}$　　　C. $\frac{4}{9}$ and 46%

   D. 0.66 and $\frac{2}{3}$　　　E. 0.43 and $\frac{3}{7}$　　　F. $\frac{6}{15}$ and 40%

PART 3　Computation Practice

Solve the following problems using paper and pencil. Estimate to be sure your answers are reasonable. Give your answers to division problems as mixed numbers. Use a separate sheet of paper if you need more space.

A. $87 \times 62 =$　　　B. $2.3 \times 52 =$　　　C. $1892 \div 5 =$

D. $3406 \div 27 =$　　　E. $4\frac{5}{6} + 3\frac{1}{5} =$　　　F. $\frac{11}{12} + 1\frac{2}{3} =$

G. $\frac{2}{3} \times 36 =$　　　H. $\frac{3}{5} \times \frac{5}{6} =$　　　I. $314.56 + .89 =$

J. $1089.23 - 17.9 =$　　　K. $58 - .36 =$　　　L. $173.4 + 38.65 =$

Discovery Assignment Book - page 202　(*Answers on p. 71*)

Math Facts

DPP items E and I provide practice with the division facts. Task H reviews dividing with remainders and translating the answers to mixed numbers and to decimals.

Homework and Practice

- Use DPP Task F to review translating between fractions, decimals, and percents. Students will use these skills in Part 3 of this lesson.

- Use DPP item G to provide practice with ratio and proportion. Assign Task J to review computation with time.

- Assign Part 3 of the Home Practice.

Answers for Part 3 of the Home Practice are in the Answer Key at the end of this lesson and at the end of this unit.

Assessment

Use the *Observational Assessment Record* to assess students' abilities to use ratios and proportions to solve problems.

Extension

Use the Challenge *Question 14* in the *Student Guide* as an extension.

Math Facts and Daily Practice and Problems

Use DPP items E, H, and I to review division facts. Task F reviews translating between fractions, decimals, and percents, while Task J investigates computation with time. Item G involves measurement and ratios.

Part 1. Introduction

1. Ask students to discuss the reasons they think objects sink or float.
2. Read together the vignette on the *Sink and Float* Activity Pages in the *Student Guide*.

Part 2. Collecting Mass and Volume Data

1. Students find the masses of several objects and record them in the data table on the *Sink and Float* Activity Pages in the *Discovery Assignment Book*.
2. Students find the volumes of the same objects and record them in the data table.
3. Students discuss again the reasons they think objects sink or float.

Part 3. Density

1. Review DPP Task F for practice with translating between fractions, decimals, and percents.
2. Introduce the concept of density.
3. Students write the density of the objects as ratios in the tables on the *Sink and Float Tables* Activity Page.
4. Using calculators, students compute the densities of the objects as decimals.
5. Students compute the density of water.

Part 4. Finding Patterns

Students discover the pattern that things sink in water if their mass (in grams) is greater than their volume (in cubic centimeters). In other words, they sink if their densities are greater than 1g/cc (the density of water). They apply this to solve problems *(Questions 11–12)*.

Part 5. Tying It Together

1. The class compares the density of a pound of feathers and a pound of lead. *(Question 13)*
2. Students discuss how much cargo a boat can hold before sinking. *(Question 14)*

Homework

Assign Part 3 of the Home Practice.

Assessment

Use the *Observational Assessment Record* to note students' abilities to use ratios and proportions to solve problems.

Extension

Use *Question 14* as an extension.

Answer Key is on pages 69–73.

Notes:

Mass Review

What is mass?

Mass is the amount of matter in an object. We can get an idea about the mass of an object by lifting it up. Objects that weigh more than other objects have more mass.

If we want to compare the mass of two things, we can use a two-pan balance. But before we use the balance, we should make sure it is level. You can use a small piece of clay to level your balance by placing it on the side that is higher.

Blackline Master

To measure mass, we need a unit of measure. Common metric units of mass are the gram (g) and the kilogram (kg). A kilogram is 1000 grams. So, we measure the mass of small objects in grams and the mass of large objects in kilograms.

Michael used the two-pan balance to find the mass of his calculator. His standard masses have a mass of 1 gram and 10 grams.

He found the mass was 92 grams. Can you see why?

Volume Review

The **volume** of an object is the amount of space it takes up. A common metric unit of volume is the **cubic centimeter (cc),** the volume of a cube that is one centimeter long on each side.

1 cubic centimeter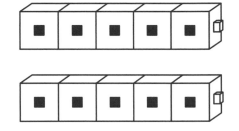

What is the total volume of these cubes?

A **milliliter (ml)** is another metric unit of volume. It is the same as 1 cubic centimeter.

A **liter (l)** is a metric unit used to measure the volume of larger objects. One liter holds 1000 milliliters; it also holds 1000 cubic centimeters.

We can estimate the volume of a rock by making a model of the rock using centimeter connecting cubes and counting the cubes.

1. Estimate the volume of the rock in the picture by counting the cubes.

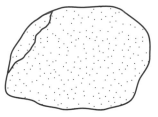 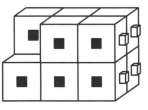

Blackline Master

Name _____   Date _____

We can also measure the volume of an object using a graduated cylinder. This method is called measuring volume by displacement because you find out how much water the object displaces or pushes away.

We can find the rock's volume by subtracting the volume of water in the graduated cylinder before adding the rock from the total volume after adding the rock.

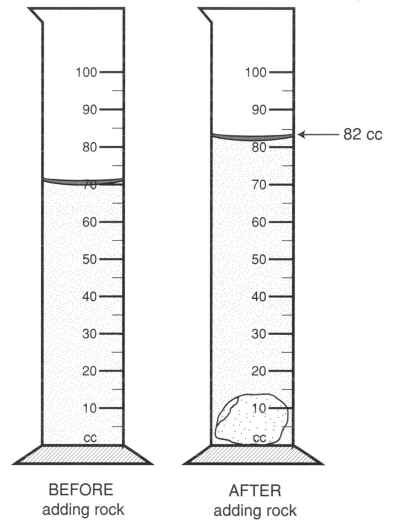

BEFORE
adding rock

AFTER
adding rock

2. What is the volume of the rock?

To read the level of water in a graduated cylinder accurately, bend down and **put your eyes at the level of the water.** In this picture, only Shanila is reading the water level correctly.

Water creeps up the sides of a graduated cylinder. It makes a curved surface at the top called a **meniscus.** (This is more noticeable in glass cylinders than in plastic ones.) The meniscus makes it look as though there are two lines on top of each other. You should always *read the lower line.* The lower line shows the level of the water. The cylinder shows a meniscus with a water level of 80 cc.

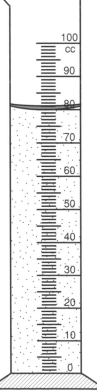

Copyright © Kendall/Hunt Publishing Company

Student Guide (p. 412)

1.–2. See Figure 8 in Lesson Guide 3 for sample data table.*

3. No. In our sample data, paraffin has more mass than the rock. But, paraffin floats in water and the rock sinks.

4. No. From the sample data table we can see that clay sinks in water. In our sample data, wood has less mass than clay and wood floats. Paraffin has more mass than clay and it also floats. Therefore, whether an object sinks or floats does not depend only on its mass.

5. See Figure 8 in Lesson Guide 3 for sample data.*

6. No. In our sample data, the piece of wood has more volume than the plastic or steel sphere. But wood floats.

7. No. From the data table we can see that clay sinks in water. In our sample data, the cork has less volume than clay and cork floats. Paraffin has more volume than clay and it also floats. Therefore, whether an object sinks or floats does not depend only on its volume.

Student Guide (p. 413)

8. **A.–B.*** See Figure 9 in Lesson Guide 3.

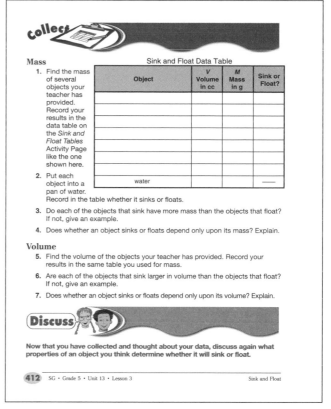

Student Guide - page 412

Student Guide - page 413

*Answers and/or discussion are included in the Lesson Guide.

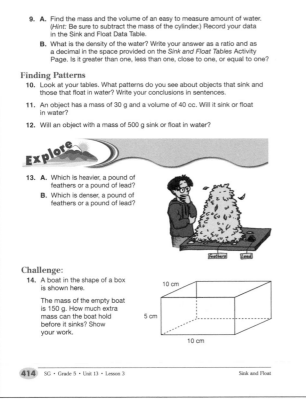

Student Guide - page 414

9.* **A.** Answers will vary.

    B. The measured density of the water will be very close to one. By definition, it is 1 g/cc.

10. Answers may vary. Possible patterns include:

If the mass of an object is larger than its volume (in cubic centimeters) then the object sinks in water; otherwise it floats. If the density of an object (in grams) is greater than $\frac{1\,g}{1\,cc}$, then the object sinks in water; otherwise it floats.*

11. Since the density of the object is $\frac{30\,g}{40\,cc} = \frac{0.75\,g}{cc}$, which is less than 1 g/cc, the object will float.*

12. We can't tell whether the object will sink or float. We need to know its volume also.*

13.* **A.** Neither one is heavier; they both weigh the same.

    B. A pound of lead is denser. Since the volume of a pound of feathers is larger than the volume of a pound of lead, the density of the feathers is smaller than the density of lead.

14. The volume of the box is 10 cm $\times$ 5 cm $\times$ 10 cm = 500 cc. The total mass of the boat (the mass of the empty boat and the mass of the load) cannot have more than 500 g. If the ratio $\frac{M}{V}$ is greater than 1, the boat will sink. Thus, as long as the extra mass is less than 350 g, the total mass will be less than 500 g and the boat will not sink.*

*Answers and/or discussion are included in the Lesson Guide.

Discovery Assignment Book (p. 202)

Home Practice*

Part 3. Computation Practice

A. 5394   B. 119.6

C. 378 R2   D. 126 R4

E. $8\frac{1}{30}$ F. $2\frac{7}{12}$

G. 24   H. $\frac{1}{2}$

I. 315.45   J. 1071.33

K. 57.64   L. 212.05

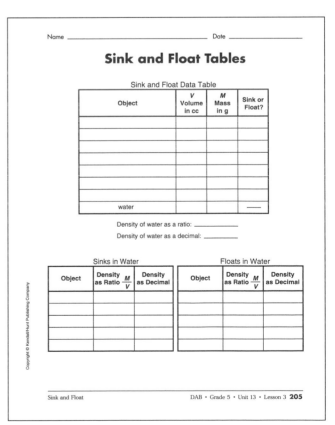

Discovery Assignment Book - page 202

Discovery Assignment Book (p. 205)

Sink and Float Tables

See Figures 8–9 in Lesson Guide 3 for sample completed tables.†

Discovery Assignment Book - page 205

*Answers for all the Home Practice in the *Discovery Assignment Book* are at the end of the unit.

†Answers and/or discussion are included in the Lesson Guide.

Unit Resource Guide - page 64

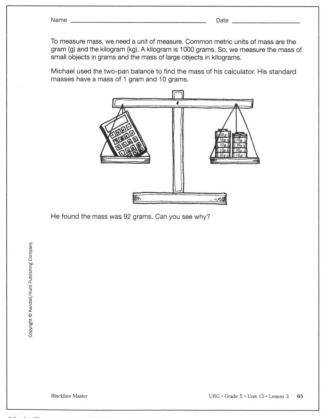

Unit Resource Guide - page 65

Unit Resource Guide (pp. 64–65)

Mass Review

Michael used nine 10-gram masses, which equal 90 grams, and two 1-gram masses, which equal 2 grams, for a total of 92 grams.

Unit Resource Guide (pp. 66–67)

Volume Review

1. 11 cc

2. 12 cc; $82 - 70 = 12$ cc

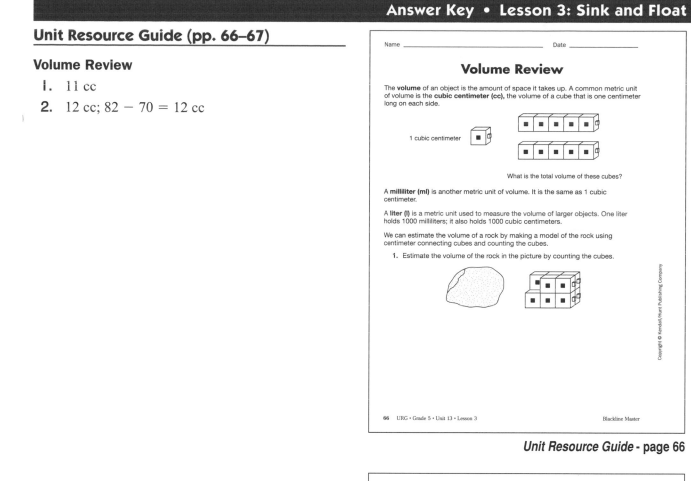

Unit Resource Guide - page 66

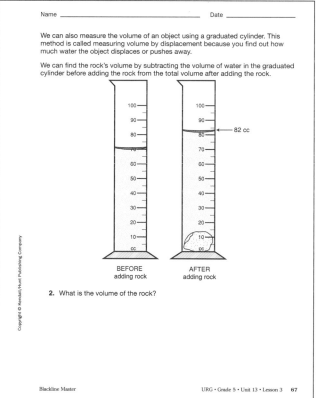

Unit Resource Guide - page 67

Lesson 4

Mass vs. Volume: Proportions and Density

Lesson Overview

Estimated Class Sessions

4-5

Students find the mass and volume of different amounts of clay and different-sized steel spheres. They graph their data and obtain straight lines through (0, 0). This leads them to conclude that the density of a material does not change when different amounts of the same material are measured. It also enables them to use proportional reasoning to solve problems about mass and volume. As an extension, students explore sinking and floating in different liquids and explain such mysteries as why eggs float in salt water but not in tap water.

Key Content

- Using numerical variables.
- Drawing and interpreting best-fit lines.
- Collecting, organizing, graphing, and analyzing data.
- Measuring mass.
- Measuring volume.
- Translating between different representations of ratios (graphical and symbolic).
- Using patterns in tables and graphs to make predictions and solve problems.
- Using ratios and proportions to solve problems.

- Translating between graphs and real-world events.
- Connecting mathematics and science to real-world events: investigating why objects sink or float.

Key Vocabulary

- density
- extrapolation
- interpolation
- variables in proportion

Math Facts

DPP items M and Q review division facts.

Homework

Assign homework *Questions 1–7* in the *Student Guide*.

Assessment

1. Assign Home Practice Part 4.
2. Grade the lab by assigning points to each part.
3. Use the *Observational Assessment Record* to assess students' abilities to measure mass and volume.
4. Transfer appropriate documentation from the Unit 13 *Observational Assessment Record* to students' *Individual Assessment Record Sheets*.

Materials List

Supplies and Copies

Student	Teacher
Supplies for Each Student Group	**Supplies**
• 5 $\frac{1}{2}$-inch-diameter steel spheres • 1-inch-diameter steel sphere • 1$\frac{1}{4}$-inch-diameter steel sphere • enough clay to make 3 pieces about the same size as the steel spheres and a small piece for leveling the balance; (clay cannot be water soluble) • two-pan balance • set of gram masses • 250-cc graduated cylinder • 100-cc graduated cylinder • paper towels • eyedropper • water • cup or beaker for pouring water • calculator • vegetable oil, corn syrup, clear soda, raisins, eggs, salt, and food coloring for the extension	
Copies	**Copies/Transparencies**
• 2 copies of *Centimeter Graph Paper* per student (*Unit Resource Guide* Page 34) • 2 copies of *Three-column Data Table* per student (*Unit Resource Guide* Page 91)	• 2 transparencies of *Centimeter Graph Paper* (*Unit Resource Guide* Page 34)

All blackline masters including assessment, transparency, and DPP masters are also on the Teacher Resource CD.

Student Books
Mass vs. Volume: Proportions and Density (*Student Guide* Pages 415–422)
Completed Sink and Float Data Table (*Discovery Assignment Book* Page 205)

Daily Practice and Problems and Home Practice
DPP items K–R (*Unit Resource Guide* Pages 18–22)
Home Practice Part 4 (*Discovery Assignment Book* Page 203)

Note: Classrooms whose pacing differs significantly from the suggested pacing of the units should use the Math Facts Calendar in Section 4 of the *Facts Resource Guide* to ensure students receive the complete math facts program.

Assessment Tools
Observational Assessment Record (*Unit Resource Guide* Pages 11–12)
Individual Assessment Record Sheet (*Teacher Implementation Guide,* Assessment section)

Daily Practice and Problems

Suggestions for using the DPPs are on pages 84–85.

K. Bit: Analogies (URG p. 18)

Use the comparison on the left to complete the comparison on the right.

A. 0.5 is to $\frac{1}{2}$ as 0.75 is to _____.

B. Millimeter is to meter as milliliter is to _____.

C. 180° is to triangle as 360° is to _____.

D. Centimeter is to length as square centimeter is to _____.

L. Task: Sums of Angles (URG p. 19)

A. Draw a triangle with one 50° angle and one 90° angle. What is the measure of the third angle? What is the sum of all three angles?

B. Draw a quadrilateral with one 105° angle and one 90° angle. What are the measures of your other two angles? What is the sum of all four angles?

M. Bit: Facts (URG p. 19)

Find the value of n that makes these number sentences true.

A. $50 \div 5 = n$ B. $n \div 3 = 5$

C. $36 \div n = 6$ D. $40 \div 20 = n$

E. $700 \div 10 = n$ F. $n \div 5 = 5$

G. $81 \div n = 9$ H. $200 \div 2 = n$

I. $n \div 7 = 2$ J. $35 \div n = 5$

N. Task: Working with Large Numbers (URG p. 20)

1. Use paper and pencil or mental math to solve the following. Estimate to be sure your answers are reasonable.

A. $3467 + 9246 =$ B. $5000 - 4839 =$

C. $100 \times 2.5 =$ D. $28,468 \div 9 =$

E. $549 \times 0.3 =$ F. $13,047 \div 28 =$

2. Explain your strategies for Questions 1B and 1C.

O. Bit: Making Goop! (URG p. 20)

To make enough goop for 4 students to play with, mix 1 part water, 3 parts flour, and 5 parts salt.

If I have:

A. 8 students, how many parts of salt will I need?

B. 9 parts flour, how many parts of salt will I need?

C. 25 parts salt, how many students will have goop?

D. $\frac{1}{2}$ part water, how many parts of salt and flour do I need?

P. Challenge: A Probability Riddle (URG p. 21)

The answer to this riddle is the name of one of the states of the United States of America. Use these clues to help you determine how many of each letter are in the state's name. Then rearrange the letters to form the name.

The probability of choosing the letter:

O is $\frac{1}{8}$ I is $\frac{3}{8}$ S is $\frac{1}{8}$ L is $\frac{1}{4}$ N is $\frac{1}{8}$

Q. Bit: Using the Facts (URG p. 21)

Try to solve the following in your head.

A. $102 \div 10 =$ B. $13 \div 2 =$

C. $39 \div 5 =$ D. $37 \div 6 =$

E. $84 \div 9 =$ F. $63 \div 6 =$

R. Challenge: Theo the Tutor (URG p. 22)

A. If Theo earns $10.00 for $2\frac{1}{2}$ hours of tutoring, what is his hourly rate?

B. If Theo needs $57.50 to buy a video game, how many hours will he need to tutor?

C. If Theo tutors 5 hours per week, how much money will he earn after 6 weeks of tutoring?

Teaching the Lab

Part 1 Beginning the Investigation and Drawing the Picture

In Lesson 3 *Sink and Float,* students investigated the mass and volume of objects and found they can use the ratio of mass to volume **(density)** to predict whether an object will sink or float. Read together the vignette in the *Mass vs. Volume: Proportions and Density* Lab Pages in the *Student Guide,* in which students in Mr. Moreno's class wonder whether different amounts of the same material have the same density. They decide to do an experiment to find out.

In this experiment, students measure the mass and volume of three different amounts of the same material and determine a relationship between these two variables. They actually carry out two experiments, one for clay and one for steel, and plot the data on the same graph.

Before beginning the experiment, students should draw a picture of what they will be doing *(Question 1).* They should show all the equipment they will use and label the variables. A sample picture is shown in Figure 10.

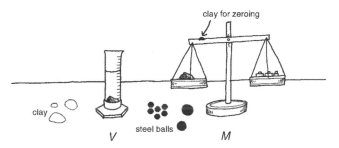

Figure 10: *A sample picture of the experiment*

Part 2 Collecting Data

Students should measure as accurately as possible. It is difficult to obtain accurate results when measuring small objects. When measuring volume the objects should be big enough to raise the water level in the graduated cylinder by at least one division. The smallest steel ball ($\frac{1}{2}$-inch diameter) is not big enough to do that. So, students find the volume of 5 steel balls and divide the answer by 5. They can do the same when finding mass.

The clay balls need to be different enough in size to spread out the data points on the graph. To graph the data for steel and clay on the same graph with the same scale, the three clay lumps should be about the same size as the steel balls. Since it is hard to make

---

Mass vs. Volume: Proportions and Density

Mr. Moreno's class is experimenting with things that sink and float.

"This piece of clay sinks in water," observed Romesh. "I'll try a smaller piece. That will be lighter, so maybe it will float."

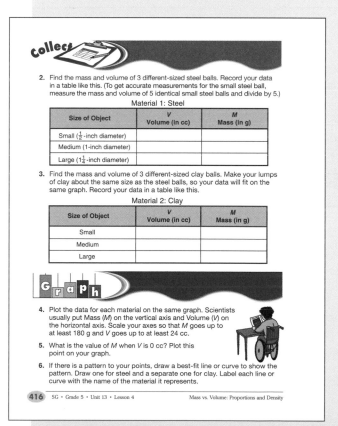

"I'm not sure," said Ana. "A smaller piece would have less mass, but wouldn't it have less volume too? Maybe its density wouldn't be different."

"We can do an experiment to find out whether a different amount of the same material has a different density," said Mr. Moreno.

The students measured the mass and volume of 3 different amounts of clay, recorded their data in a data table, and graphed their data. Then they did the same thing for different amounts of steel to see whether they got similar results for different materials. In the lab that follows, you will do the same.

Draw

You will find the mass and volume of 3 steel balls your teacher gives you and 3 lumps of clay you make about the same size as the steel balls.

1. Discuss with your group how you will do the experiment. Then draw a picture that shows what you will do. Be sure to label the variables and include all the equipment you will use.

Mass vs. Volume: Proportions and Density   SG • Grade 5 • Unit 13 • Lesson 4   415

Student Guide - page 415 (Answers on p. 92)

Collect

2. Find the mass and volume of 3 different-sized steel balls. Record your data in a table like this. (To get accurate measurements for the small steel ball, measure the mass and volume of 5 identical small steel balls and divide by 5.)

Material 1: Steel

Size of Object	V Volume (in cc)	M Mass (in g)
Small ($\frac{1}{2}$-inch diameter)		
Medium (1-inch diameter)		
Large (1$\frac{1}{4}$-inch diameter)		

3. Find the mass and volume of 3 different-sized clay balls. Make your lumps of clay about the same size as the steel balls, so your data will fit on the same graph. Record your data in a table like this.

Material 2: Clay

Size of Object	V Volume (in cc)	M Mass (in g)
Small		
Medium		
Large		

Graph

4. Plot the data for each material on the same graph. Scientists usually put Mass (*M*) on the vertical axis and Volume (*V*) on the horizontal axis. Scale your axes so that *M* goes up to at least 180 g and *V* goes up to at least 24 cc.

5. What is the value of *M* when *V* is 0 cc? Plot this point on your graph.

6. If there is a pattern to your points, draw a best-fit line or curve to show the pattern. Draw one for steel and a separate one for clay. Label each line or curve with the name of the material it represents.

416   SG • Grade 5 • Unit 13 • Lesson 4   Mass vs. Volume: Proportions and Density

Student Guide - page 416 (Answers on p. 92)

5 identical small balls of clay, make the small clay ball a little larger than the small steel sphere, about 2 to 4 cc. Have students find the volume and mass of steel and clay balls and record their data on a *Three-column Data Table (Questions 2–3)*. Sample data are shown in Figure 11.

Part 3 Graphing the Data

Scientists usually plot volume on the horizontal axis and mass on the vertical axis. This way, the density, $\frac{M}{V}$, corresponds to the steepness of the line (the denser the object, the steeper the line).

Students plot their data for each material on the same graph *(Question 4)* so they can make comparisons. Notice that the point (0, 0) should be included as a data point on the graph *(Question 5)*. This is because an object with 0 volume has 0 mass; in other words, $M = 0$ g when $V = 0$ cc.

Students' data points should show a straight-line pattern. They then draw a best-fit line through their data. They will have two different lines, one for steel and one for clay. A graph of our sample data is shown in Figure 12. You can review how to draw a best-fit line

- Be sure students use the same lumps of clay when they measure mass as when they measure volume. Measure the mass of the clay before the volume, to avoid soggy clay.
- Be sure students record only the volume of the objects, and not the volume of the water and the objects combined.

Material 1: Steel

Size of Object	V Volume (in cc)	M Mass (in g)
Small (½-inch diameter)	1.1	8.4
Medium (1-inch diameter)	8.5	66
Large (1¼-inch diameter)	16.5	130

Material 2: Clay

Size of Object	V Volume (in cc)	M Mass (in g)
Small	2	4
Medium	9.5	19
Large	21	45

Figure 11: *Sample data*

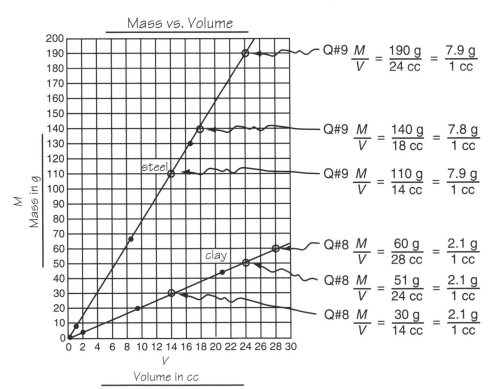

Figure 12: *Graph of sample data*

by plotting these data points on a transparency. You can then use this transparency when discussing the Explore questions.

The fact that the mass vs. volume graph of a material is a straight line through (0, 0) is important. This means that the ratio of mass to volume (density) is the same for any amount of material. It also means proportional reasoning can be used to solve problems about mass and volume, as in *Questions 14–15*.

Part 4 Exploring the Data

After students collect their data and make their graphs, they are ready to work on the questions. *Question 7* provides straightforward practice in reading the graph. Students' answers may vary a little because of variations in their data and their best-fit lines. Remind them that you expect their answers to come from their own graphs. Consistency with their data is important; matching the answers of a neighbor (or even our sample data) is not as important. Of course, answers that are far from other people's answers probably indicate an error in method or measurement and should be reexamined. If inaccurate data is suspected, students should collect their data again.

Question 8 asks students to choose a total of three different points on the line for clay and use them to write ratios of mass to volume. Figure 12 shows three such ratios. When each ratio is written as a unit ratio rounded to the nearest tenth, we find that they are all approximately equal to 2.1 g/cc. Following the same procedure for steel in *Question 9,* we find that the ratios are approximately equal to 7.9 g/cc.

In *Question 10,* students examine their results to answer Romesh's original questions. The results for *Question 8* lead students to the idea that the ratio of mass to volume ($\frac{M}{V}$) for clay will be the same for any values of M and V chosen from points on the line for clay. Similarly, the ratio of mass to volume ($\frac{M}{V}$) will be the same for steel for any values of M and V chosen from points on the line for steel *(Question 9).* But this ratio is density! Therefore, the density is the same for different amounts of the same material *(Question 10A).* Students can verify this by computing the densities using different points on their lines. Since changing the size doesn't change the density, it also doesn't change whether the material sinks or floats. Thus a smaller piece of clay will not float *(Question 10B)*—it has the same density as the larger piece (which sinks).

Question 11 asks students to give the densities using their data. They should compute the densities from their lines, not their raw data. The individual data

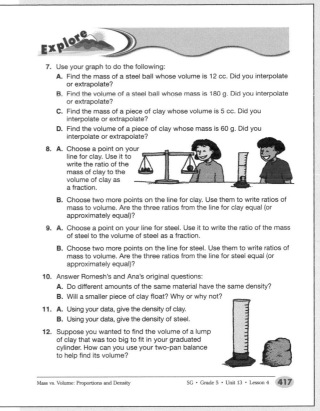

Student Guide - page 417 *(Answers on p. 93)*

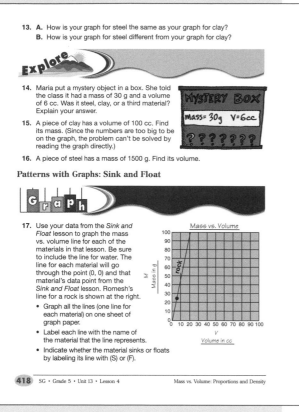

Student Guide - page 418 *(Answers on p. 94)*

points may give slightly different values of $\frac{M}{V}$ due to inevitable measurement error. A best-fit line averages out measurement error. For this reason the best-fit line gives a value for the density that is more accurate than any of the individual data points (unless they are on the line). For the same reason, the values you get for the densities of steel and clay may not be the same as those we found in *Sink and Float*. Of course, they should be close.

Using our graph, we selected points that are easy to read. These points are circled in Figure 12. From this, we compute that the density of clay is $\frac{M}{V} = \frac{2.1\,\text{g}}{1\,\text{cc}}$. Similarly, we compute that the density of steel is $\frac{7.9\,\text{g}}{1\,\text{cc}}$. Students' values should be similar.

The two experiments, one for steel and one for clay, show us that density depends on the material. The lines for steel and clay were different. Two different materials will rarely have the same density, or equivalently, the same mass-volume line. Measuring density or graphing the mass vs. volume line of a material can help to identify the material. This idea is applied in **Question 14.** Maria's mystery object has a density of $\frac{30\,\text{g}}{6\,\text{cc}}$, or $\frac{5\,\text{g}}{1\,\text{cc}}$. This is less than the density of steel (about $\frac{7.9\,\text{g}}{1\,\text{cc}}$) and more than the density of clay (about $\frac{2.1\,\text{g}}{1\,\text{cc}}$). So the material can't be either steel or clay. Graphically, the point *(V, M)* = (6, 30) does not fall on the line for steel or clay, so the material must be a third substance.

In **Question 15,** students are asked to find the mass of 100 cc of clay. This can be done in several ways. One way is to use the line for clay on their graphs to obtain the density of clay. They can use the density to write a proportion involving the mass and volume of clay and then solve this proportion to find their answer. Different student groups will have different numbers in their proportions, but the ratios should be about the same. Using our sample graph, we choose a point where the best-fit line meets two grid lines, because it is easier to read accurately. We choose $M = 30$ g and $V = 14$ cc. Thus, the density is $\frac{30\,\text{g}}{14\,\text{cc}}$ and our proportion is:

$$\frac{M}{V} = \frac{30\text{ g}}{14\text{ cc}}$$

To find *M* when *V* = 100 cc, we need to solve the proportion:

$$\frac{M}{100\text{ cc}} = \frac{30\text{ g}}{14\text{ cc}}$$

The numbers are a little messy here because they come from real data, but we can use what we know about equivalent fractions to help us solve the proportion. We know that the numerators are related by the same factor as the denominators. By what factor can we multiply 14 cc (the denominator on the right) to get 100 cc (the denominator on the left)? The answer is 100 ÷ 14, or about 7.14. Thus, we can multiply the numerator on the right, 30 g, by the same factor, 7.14, to get M, the numerator on the left. Therefore, $M \approx 7.14 \times 30$ g = 214 g. Note, if students estimate that 100 ÷ 14 is about 7, they would compute that the mass is about 7×30 g or about 210 g. Given that there is a certain amount of measurement error, this estimate is acceptable.

$$\overset{\times\,7.14}{\underset{\times\,7.14}{\frac{M}{100\text{ cc}} = \frac{30\text{ g}}{14\text{ cc}}}}$$

Another way to solve the proportion is to replace $\frac{30\text{ g}}{14\text{ cc}}$ by a unit ratio. Since 30 ÷ 14 ≈ 2.1, we need to solve:

$$\frac{M}{100\text{ cc}} = \frac{2.1\text{ g}}{1\text{ cc}}$$

If 1 cc has a mass of about 2.1 g, then 100 cc will have a mass of about 100×2.1 g or 210 g.

A third method of solving the problem in *Question 15* is to read the volume of a smaller mass that is on the graph and then multiply by an appropriate number to find the volume of the given mass. Although the value $V = 100$ cc is not on their graph, $V = 25$ cc is. From our graph, the mass of a 25-cc piece of clay is about $M = 54$ g. A piece of clay that has four times the volume, 100 cc, would have four times the mass as well. Therefore, the mass would be 4×54 g = 216 g. Using the different methods, the answers are about the same. Your students' answers will vary slightly, based on differences in their data and graphs.

Question 16 is similar to *Question 15,* but this time the mass is known and students are asked to find the volume. One way to solve the problem is to read the ratio $\frac{M}{V}$ from the graph for steel and solve the proportion:

$$\frac{1500\text{ g}}{V} = \frac{110\text{ g}}{14\text{ cc}}$$

A second way is to read the volume of a suitable smaller mass and multiply. The value $M = 1500$ g is not on our graph. A good value on the graph to choose for M is 150 g, since 1500 g is a nice multiple of 150 g. From our graph, when M is 150 g, V is about 19 cc. A piece of steel that has 10 times the mass, 1500 g, would have 10 times the volume as well.

Therefore, we conclude that $V \approx 10 \times 19$ cc $= 190$ cc. Again, your students' answers will vary slightly because of differences in their data and graphs.

Part 5 Patterns with Graphs: Sink and Float

Students now graph the mass vs. volume lines for each material they investigated in Lesson 3 *Sink and Float (Question 17).* They can use the data from that activity to plot the lines. From their graphs for clay and steel in Part 3, they learned that each material has its own line and it passes through (0, 0). Since that is true, they only need one data point, along with (0, 0), to determine a material's line. (Plotting more data points would improve the accuracy, but is not needed for our purposes.) They should plot the lines on one sheet of graph paper, label each line, and indicate whether the material sinks or floats, as shown in Figure 13. Students will probably need to use a new sheet of graph paper since the data from Lesson 3 will probably not fit on the *Mass vs. Volume* graph they made for clay and steel. Students can use one color to draw lines for objects that sink, another color for objects that float, and a third color for the line for water. You may want to demonstrate how to do this by graphing a few lines on a transparency.

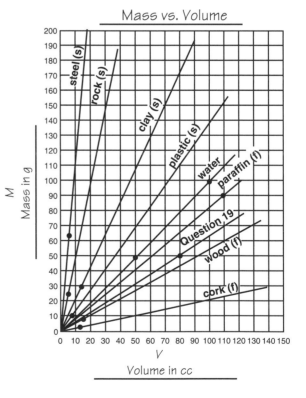

Figure 13: *Mass vs. volume lines for several materials*

The students should recognize a pattern *(Question 18):* The lines of objects that sink lie above the line for water. The lines of objects that float lie below the line for water.

18. What pattern do you see in your graph? Explain how to tell from your graph whether an object will sink or float.

19. On your graph, plot the data point for a mystery object with a mass of 50 g and a volume of 80 cc. Draw the line through this point and the point $M = 0$, $V = 0$, representing the mass vs. volume line for this material. (Label it "Question 19.")

   A. Based on the pattern you observed in your graph, would you expect the object to sink or float in water? Explain.

   B. Find the object's density. Based on its density, would you expect the object to sink or float in water? Explain.

20. A. Explain how to use the mass and volume data table to compare densities.

   B. Explain how to use the graph to compare densities.

21. The final product from a steel mill should not have air pockets trapped inside. You are given a piece of steel with a volume of 20 cc. Explain how you would go about determining whether the piece was solid steel or had air trapped inside.

22. Two rocks are thought to be made of the same material. Explain how you could investigate whether this is true.

23. An object has a density of $\frac{4 \text{ g}}{1 \text{ cc}}$ or 4 g/cc.

   A. If its volume is 80 cc, what is its mass? Show your work.

   B. If its mass is 100 g, what is its volume? Show your work.

Mass vs. Volume: Proportions and Density　　SG • Grade 5 • Unit 13 • Lesson 4　**419**

Student Guide - page 419 (Answers on p. 94)

In **Question 19,** students apply patterns they observed to determine whether an object sinks or floats. They use the pattern with graphs from this lesson and the pattern with densities from the previous lesson. They plot the data point for $V = 80$ cc and $M = 50$ g. In **Question 19A,** they observe that the line for this material is below the water line and so the object floats. In **Question 19B,** they compute the density directly: $\frac{M}{V} = \frac{50 \text{ g}}{80 \text{ cc}}$ or $\frac{0.625 \text{ g}}{1 \text{ cc}}$. Since this is less than 1 g/cc (the density of water), the object floats.

In **Question 20,** students describe two ways to compare the density of materials. One way is to compute the ratio $\frac{M}{V}$ of the materials using values of M and V in the data table *(Question 20A).* Using a calculator to find a unit ratio makes comparison easier. In **Question 20B,** they describe a graphical way to compare densities. A steeper line represents more mass per volume than a line that is not as steep. Hence, it represents a material that is denser.

In **Questions 21–23** students describe how comparing densities can help to identify the material an object is composed of. Some students may choose to represent the density as a ratio and solve their problems by comparing ratios; others may choose to solve them graphically by comparing the steepness of the appropriate mass vs. volume line.

One way to solve **Question 23** is to use a proportion. The object has density $\frac{M}{V} = \frac{4 \text{ g}}{1 \text{ cc}}$. If its volume is 80 cc, we can find its mass *(Question 23A)* by solving the proportion:

$$\frac{M}{80 \text{ cc}} = \frac{4 \text{ g}}{1 \text{ cc}}$$

Since the denominator on the left is 80 times the one on the right, the numerator on the left must be 80 times the one on the right. Therefore $M = 80 \times 4$ g $= 320$ g.

$$\overset{\times 80}{\frac{M}{80 \text{ cc}} = \frac{4 \text{ g}}{1 \text{ cc}}}_{\times 80}$$

After answering the question, students can read the story of Archimedes and the King's Gold Crown in the *Student Guide.* This well-known story tells how Archimedes used density to prove that the King's crown was not pure gold.

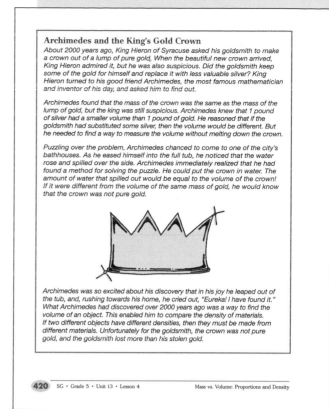

Student Guide - page 420

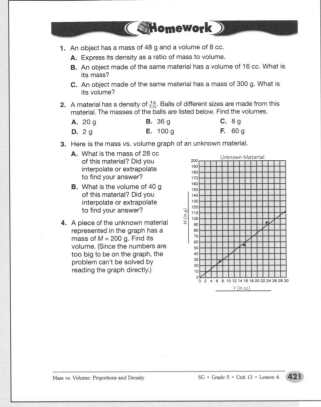

Homework

1. An object has a mass of 48 g and a volume of 8 cc.
   A. Express its density as a ratio of mass to volume.
   B. An object made of the same material has a volume of 16 cc. What is its mass?
   C. An object made of the same material has a mass of 300 g. What is its volume?

2. A material has a density of $\frac{48 \text{ g}}{3 \text{ cc}}$. Balls of different sizes are made from this material. The masses of the balls are listed below. Find the volumes.
   A. 20 g   B. 36 g   C. 8 g
   D. 2 g   E. 100 g   F. 60 g

3. Here is the mass vs. volume graph of an unknown material.
   A. What is the mass of 28 cc of this material? Did you interpolate or extrapolate to find your answer?
   B. What is the volume of 40 g of this material? Did you interpolate or extrapolate to find your answer?

4. A piece of the unknown material represented in the graph has a mass of $M = 200$ g. Find its volume. (Since the numbers are too big to be on the graph, the problem can't be solved by reading the graph directly.)

Mass vs. Volume: Proportions and Density   SG • Grade 5 • Unit 13 • Lesson 4   **421**

5. Copy the following table. Then find the density of the objects in the table. Which object has greatest density?

Object	Volume of Object (in cc)	Mass of Object (in g)	Density in g/cc
A	24	11.0	
B	9	11.0	
C	4	5.5	
D	11	5.5	

6. Here is a graph of the mass vs. volume of several materials. Using the graph, tell which of the materials will sink and which will float in water. Explain why.

7. A. Compute the densities of the materials in the graph.
   B. Based on their densities, tell which materials will sink and which will float in water. Explain why.

422   SG • Grade 5 • Unit 13 • Lesson 4   Mass vs. Volume: Proportions and Density

Math Facts

DPP items M and Q provide practice with division facts.

Homework and Practice

• Assign homework *Questions 1–7* in the *Student Guide*.

• DPP items K, L, N, and O provide practice with number sense, angle measure, computation, and proportions.

Assessment

• Use the *Observational Assessment Record* in the *Unit Resource Guide* to record student success in measuring objects' mass and volume. Transfer appropriate documentation to students' *Individual Assessment Record Sheets*.

• To grade the lab, assign a given number of points to each part and grade each part based on the following criteria:

1. Drawing the picture
   Is the procedure clearly illustrated?
   Are the variables labeled?

2. Collecting and recording the data
   Are the data organized in a data table?
   Are the columns in the data table labeled correctly?
   Are the data reasonable?
   Are the correct units of measure included in the data table?

3. Graphing the data
   Does the graph have a title?
   Are the axes scaled correctly and labeled clearly?
   Did the student plot mass on the vertical axis and volume on the horizontal axis?
   Did the student use a ruler to draw accurate best-fit lines?
   Did the student correctly use the lines to answer Explore *Questions 7 and 8?*
   Did the student show any interpolation or extrapolation on the graph?

4. Solving the problems
   Are the answers correct based on the data?
   Are the answers, including the explanations, clear and complete?

- Use the homework questions as an assessment. Advise students that you will use the Student Rubrics: *Knowing* to score their answers to **Question 4** and *Telling* to score their answers to **Question 7.** Ask students to review the student rubrics in the *Student Guide.* Score their responses using the Knowing and Telling dimensions of the *TIMS Multidimensional Rubric* in the Assessment section of the *Teacher Implementation Guide.*

- Assign Home Practice Part 4 as an assessment.

Answers for Part 4 of the Home Practice are in the Answer Key at the end of this lesson and at the end of this unit.

Extension

- DPP items P and R challenge students with a probability riddle and problems involving money.

- If there is time, we highly recommend choosing some of the activities that follow. All of them can be considered science activities. Some seem like magic at first and the class will have fun watching and then explaining what they see. Activities can be done as teacher-led demonstrations, or assign student groups different activities from the list to present to the class. They can explain why their "trick" isn't really magic, but just an application of density.

1. Margarine Tub Boats

Students can use their knowledge of mass, volume, and density to predict how much mass a boat can hold before sinking. One way to do this is to use margarine tubs as boats. Students can determine the volume of the "boat" using a graduated cylinder and water. Since the walls of the margarine tub are relatively thin, the capacity, or inside volume, of the tub will provide a close estimate of the boat's total volume. (However, if you cut the tub into small strips, you can find its volume using a graduated cylinder and water. Adding the volume of the tub to its inside volume, or capacity, will give the total volume of the tub.) Once students know the boat's volume, they can apply what they learned in *Sink and Float* and *Mass vs. Volume: Proportions and Density* to predict the maximum amount of mass the boat can hold. They can test their prediction by first measuring the mass of the empty boat and then carefully filling the floating tub with standard masses until the boat sinks. If the students

---

Name _____ Date _____

PART 4 **Measuring the Density of Rocks**
You will need a piece of graph paper to complete these questions.

1. On a geology field trip, Blanca found three rocks made of the same type of material. She measured the mass and volume of each rock. Her data table is shown at the right. Plot the data on a piece of graph paper. Put Mass (*M*) on the vertical axis and Volume (*V*) on the horizontal axis. Scale your axes so that *M* goes up to 100 g and *V* goes up to 30 cc.

Rock	Volume (cc)	Mass (g)
A	3	8.5
B	5	15
C	21	60

2. Use a point on the line to find the density for this kind of rock. Express the density as a ratio of mass to volume.

3. Remember, the density of water is $\frac{1g}{1cc}$ (or 1 g/cc). Compare the density of Blanca's rocks with the density of water. Would you expect the rocks to sink or float? Why?

4. On the field trip, Blanca also found a bigger rock of the same material. This rock is too big to fit in the graduated cylinder. She knows the mass of the rock is 80 grams. Use your graph to find the volume of this rock.

5. A rock made of the same material has a volume of 15 cc. What is its mass? Explain how you found your answer.

6. If a rock made of the same material has a volume of 40 cc, what is its mass? Show your solution strategy.

RATIO AND PROPORTION   DAB • Grade 5 • Unit 13 **203**

Discovery Assignment Book - page 203 (Answers on p. 97)

made careful measurements, the total mass (in grams) of the empty boat plus the largest "load" of standard masses it can hold without sinking will be close to the volume of the boat in cubic centimeters. This would keep the density of the boat with its load approximately 1.0 g/cc, the density of water. (Note: Measurements that are within 10% should be considered reasonable.) This can be represented mathematically by the following equation:

$$\frac{\text{Mass of Margarine Tub} + \text{Mass of "Load"}}{\text{Total Volume of the Boat}} \approx 1 \text{ g/cc}$$

See the discussion in Lesson Guide 3 of **Question 14** on the *Sink and Float* Activity Pages in the *Student Guide.* See the Content Note: Why Do Boats Float? in Lesson Guide 3 as well.

2. Floating in Different Liquids: A Density Mystery

So far, students have considered sinking and floating only in water. What happens if you change the type of liquid? Liquids other than water are often messy to handle and can be expensive to buy for the entire class. For this reason, you might prefer to do a classroom demonstration.

A. Determine the density of vegetable oil and corn syrup. Since this is very messy, you might prefer to use our data (see Figure 14). We found our vegetable oil to have a density of 0.9 g/cc and our corn syrup to have a density of 1.4 g/cc. (When finding the mass, don't forget to subtract the mass of the container.)

B. Ask students to add the mass vs. volume lines for these liquids to their graphs that show the Sink and Float pattern (see Figure 15). The line for syrup is above the line for water and the line for vegetable oil should be below. This means the corn syrup is denser and will sink in water and the vegetable oil is less dense and will float in water.

C. Have students predict what will happen when vegetable oil, water (with a few drops of food coloring added for a dramatic effect), and corn syrup are poured into the same container. (Ask them whether a liquid could float on another liquid.) Pour vegetable oil, then colored water, then corn syrup into a jar. The vegetable oil, although initially on the bottom, rises to the top. The corn syrup sinks to the bottom.

Object	M Mass (in g)	V Volume (in cc)	Density in g/cc
vegetable oil	27	30	.9
corn syrup	41	30	1.4

Figure 14: *Vegetable oil and corn syrup data*

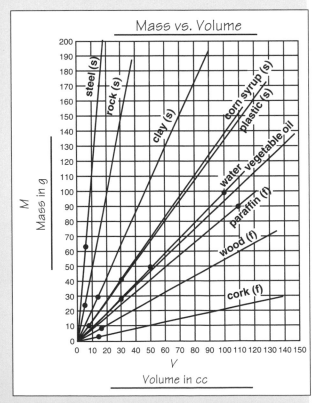

Figure 15: *Adding the data for vegetable oil and corn syrup*

D. Ask students to predict which objects from the *Sink and Float* lesson will sink and which will float in each liquid. The patterns they used for water can be generalized to other liquids: an object floats in a liquid if its density is less than the density of the liquid. Equivalently, it floats if its mass-volume line is below the line for the liquid. Students should use their data or their graphs to make their predictions.

E. Drop the objects into the jar (if an object such as paraffin won't fit into the container, break off a small piece). Students will find, for example, that the plastic sphere that sinks in water now floats in syrup. Some crayons float in water but sink in vegetable oil.

F. You can ask students to continue this activity at home. Ask them to check for objects that float in water but not oil, in syrup but not water (a grape is an example of the latter), etc. Ask them to draw a picture of the liquids and objects as they appear in their jars.

3. Mystery of the Floating Egg

A. Put an uncooked egg in tap water. It sinks.

B. Now remove the egg and dissolve salt in the water. It works well to use a ratio of about 20 cc of salt to 150 cc of water, or about 6 teaspoons of salt to 1 cup of water. Stir the salt into the water until it all dissolves completely.

C. Put the egg in the salt water. It floats. Why? Have you changed the mass or volume of the egg? No. Have you changed the volume of the water? Not much; when the salt dissolves in the water, the salt molecules fit in among the water molecules, but the volume of the mixture does not change much. But adding the salt does increase the mass of the solution. Adding salt increases the numerator in the density, $\frac{M}{V}$. Increasing the numerator gives a bigger ratio, hence a greater density. Salt water is denser than tap water. In fact it is a little denser than the egg. Thus, the egg floats.

D. You can make the lesson more quantitative by having students measure the mass and volume of the egg and the salt water and compute the density of each. The density of our egg was 1.07 g/cc (we measured M = 60 g and V = 56 cc). With about 20 cc of salt per 150 cc of water, our salt water had a density of 1.08 g/cc. The density of our egg was less than the density of the salt water, so it floated.

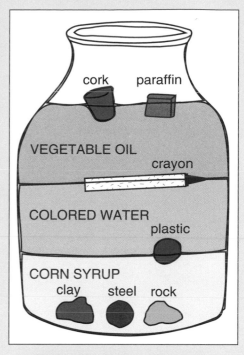

Figure 16: *Objects floating at different levels*

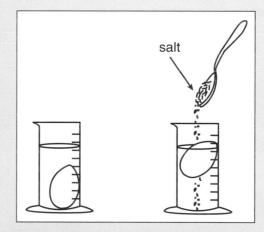

Figure 17: *An egg sinking in tap water and floating in salt water*

E. During the demonstration, you can use the following discussion prompts:

- *Which is denser, the water or the egg?* (The egg, because it sinks in water.)

- *Which is denser, the salt water or the egg?* (The salt water, because the egg floats in it.)

- *When salt is dissolved in water, the molecules of salt are packed in among the molecules of water, so the volume does not change much. However, the mass does change. How does this affect the density of the solution?* (When M is greater, $\frac{M}{V}$ is greater. Therefore the density is greater.)

- *Do you think it would be easier to float in fresh lake water or in salty ocean water? Ask your friends and family whether they have ever gone swimming in salt water. Did they notice a difference?* (It is much easier to float in salt water. In fact, many people are able to lie on their backs with their toes sticking out because the density of salt water makes it easier to float.)

4. Mystery of the Rising and Falling Raisin

Place a raisin (or several raisins) in a glass of clear soda. (Neither dried-out raisins nor diet soda work very well.) The raisin first sinks like a rock, then rises to the top, sinks again, and rises again for several up-down passages until it seems to get tired out and finally stays on the bottom. Why? Have children look closely at the raisin and ask them to figure it out using what they know about density. You might ask them:

- *Did the liquid change its mass or volume?*

- *Did the raisin change its mass or volume?*

Nothing happens to the liquid, so the density of the liquid does not change. Initially the density of the raisin must be greater than that of the liquid since the raisin sinks to the bottom. But then, the raisin picks up some of the gas that normally bubbles up in the soda. If students look closely, they can see the bubbles on the raisin. The added gas bubbles increase the volume of the raisin without increasing its mass, since each attached bubble has an infinitesimally small mass. This makes the density of the raisin-plus-gas less than the density of the water. The raisin with the added gas floats to the top. But when it gets to the top, the bubbles of carbon dioxide gas burst; the raisin returns to its original volume, and down it goes. The sequence is repeated several times until there is not enough gas left in the soda to "raise" the raisin. See Figure 18.

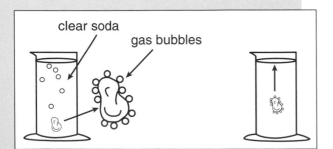

Figure 18: *A rising and falling raisin*

At a Glance

Math Facts and Daily Practice and Problems

Assign DPP items K–R. Items K and L involve geometry. Items M and Q review division facts, and N and O develop number sense. Challenge P provides a probability riddle, and Challenge R provides practice in computation with money.

Part 1. Beginning the Investigation and Drawing the Picture

1. Read together the vignette in *Mass vs. Volume: Proportions and Density* Lab Pages in the *Student Guide*.
2. Students draw pictures of what they will do in the experiment. *(Question 1)*

Part 2. Collecting Data

1. Students find the volume and mass of three sizes of steel spheres. *(Question 2)*
2. Students find the volume and mass of three lumps of clay. *(Question 3)*

Part 3. Graphing the Data

Students plot their data for steel and for clay. They get two different lines, one for steel and one for clay. *(Questions 4–6)*

Part 4. Exploring the Data

Students answer *Questions 7–16.*

Part 5. Patterns with Graphs: Sink and Float

1. Students use their data from Lesson 3, *Sink and Float,* to graph the mass vs. volume line for each of the materials in that lesson. *(Question 17)*
2. Students find a pattern in the graph and predict whether an object will sink or float. *(Question 18)*
3. Students answer *Questions 19–23,* using both graphs and ratios to compare densities.
4. Students read about Archimedes and the King's Gold Crown in the *Student Guide.*

Homework

Assign homework *Questions 1–7* in the *Student Guide.*

Assessment

1. Assign Home Practice Part 4.
2. Grade the lab by assigning points to each part.
3. Use the *Observational Assessment Record* to assess students' abilities to measure mass and volume.
4. Transfer appropriate documentation from the Unit 13 *Observational Assessment Record* to students' *Individual Assessment Record Sheets.*

At a Glance

Extension

1. Assign DPP items P and R.
2. Try one or more of the following:
   - Have students predict how much mass a margarine tub can hold before sinking.
   - Explore what happens to objects sinking and floating when you change the liquid they are in.
   - Explore why an egg floats or sinks in tap water and salt water.
   - Try sinking and floating raisins in soda water.

Answer Key is on pages 92–97.

Notes:

Name _____ Date _____

_____

Three-column Data Table, Blackline Master

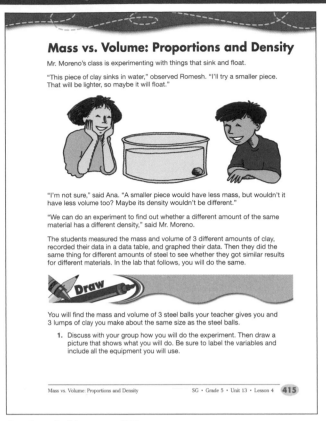

Student Guide - page 415

Student Guide (p. 415)

Mass vs. Volume: Proportions and Density

1. See Figure 10 in Lesson Guide 4 for a sample picture.*

Student Guide (p. 416)

2.–3. See Figure 11 in Lesson Guide 4 for sample data tables.*

4. See Figure 12 in Lesson Guide 4.*

5. $M = 0$ g*

6. See Figure 12 in Lesson Guide 4.*

Student Guide - page 416

*Answers and/or discussion are included in the Lesson Guide.

Student Guide (p. 417)

7. The answers are based on the sample graph,
   Figure 12 in the Lesson Guide.*

   A. About 94 g; interpolate

   B. About 23 cc; extrapolate

   C. 10 g; interpolate

   D. About 28 cc; extrapolate

8. The answers are based on the sample graph.*

   A. $\frac{M}{V} = \frac{60\,g}{28\,cc} = \frac{2.1\,g}{1\,cc}$

   B. $\frac{M}{V} = \frac{51\,g}{24\,cc} = \frac{2.1\,g}{1\,cc}$

   $\frac{M}{V} = \frac{30\,g}{14\,cc} = \frac{2.1\,g}{1\,cc}$

   All 3 ratios are equal.

9. The answers are based on the sample graph.*

   A. $\frac{M}{V} = \frac{190\,g}{24\,cc} = \frac{7.9\,g}{1\,cc}$

   B. $\frac{M}{V} = \frac{140\,g}{18\,cc} = \frac{7.8\,g}{1\,cc}$

   C. $\frac{M}{V} = \frac{110\,g}{14\,cc} = \frac{7.9\,g}{1\,cc}$

   All 3 ratios are approximately equal.

10. **A.** Yes. The density is the ratio $\frac{M}{V}$ and since this
    ratio is constant for different amounts of the
    same material, they have the same density.*

    B. No. Since the smaller piece of clay has the
    same density as the larger piece which
    sinks, the smaller piece will sink also.

11.* **A.** Using points from the sample graph as
    in Questions 8 and 9, the density of clay is
    $\frac{M}{V} = \frac{2.1\,g}{1\,cc}$.

    B. Using points from the sample graph, the
    density of steel is $\frac{M}{V} = 7.9$ g/cc.

12. We can use the balance together with our graph
    of *Mass vs. Volume* for clay to find the answer.
    We can use the two-pan balance to find the
    mass of the clay. Then, using the graph, we can
    interpolate or extrapolate to find the volume.
    Another method we can use is to represent
    density as the ratio of $\frac{M}{V}$ and compare ratios to
    find the volume.

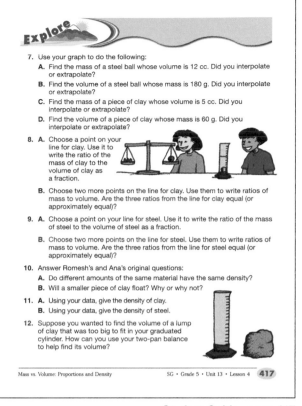

Student Guide - page 417

---

*Answers and/or discussion are included in the Lesson Guide.

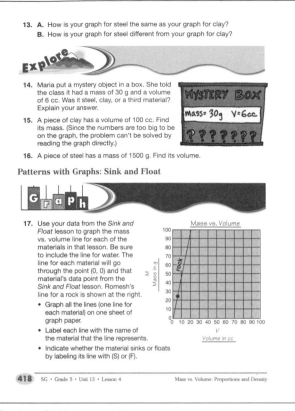

Student Guide - page 418

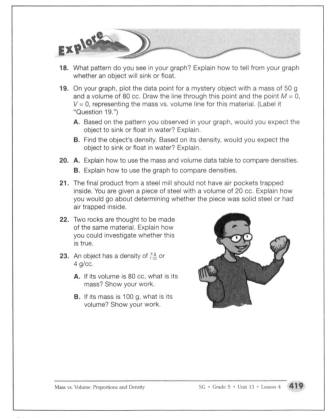

Student Guide - page 419

*Answers and/or discussion are included in the Lesson Guide.

Student Guide (p. 418)

13. **A.** Both graphs are straight lines that pass through the point (0, 0).

    B. The graph for steel is a steeper line than the graph for clay.

14. It is a third material. The mystery object has a density of $\frac{30\text{ g}}{6\text{ cc}} = 5$ g/cc. This is less than the density of steel and more than that of clay.*

15. $M \approx 214$ g or 210 g*

16. $V \approx 190$ cc*

17. See Figure 13 in Lesson Guide 4.*

Student Guide (p. 419)

18. The lines of objects that sink lie above the line for water, and the lines of objects that float lie below the line for water.*

19. **A.** Since the line for the object lies below the line for water, the object will float.*

    B. Density $= \frac{50\text{ g}}{80\text{ cc}} = 0.625$ g/cc. Since this density is less than 1 g/cc, the object will float in water.

20. **A.** Using a calculator we can compute the densities for the mass and volume given in the data table using the ratio $\frac{M}{V}$.*

    B. Graphically, a steeper line represents more mass per volume than a line that is not as steep. Therefore, a steeper line represents a material that is denser.

21. Methods may vary. We can represent density as a ratio of $\frac{M}{V}$ and compare the ratios to solve the problem.

22. We can find the density of each rock, and if they are the same, we can conclude that the rocks are probably made of the same material.

23. **A.** 320 g; $\frac{M}{80\text{ cc}} = \frac{4\text{ g}}{1\text{ cc}}$; $M = 320$ g*

    B. 25 cc; $\frac{100\text{ g}}{V} = \frac{4\text{ g}}{1\text{ cc}}$; $V = 25$ cc

Student Guide (p. 421)

Homework

1. **A.** Density $= \frac{48\,g}{8\,cc} = \frac{6\,g}{1\,cc}$

   B. 96 g; $\frac{M}{16\,cc} = \frac{6\,g}{1\,cc}$; $M = 96$ g

   C. 50 cc; $\frac{300\,g}{V} = \frac{6\,g}{1\,cc}$; $V = 50$ cc

2. These problems can be solved using the proportion $\frac{M}{V} = \frac{4\,g}{3\,cc}$.

   A. 15 cc   **B.** 27 cc

   C. 6 cc   **D.** 1.5 cc

   E. 75 cc   **F.** 45 cc

3. **A.** About 105 g, extrapolate

   B. About 10.5 cc, interpolate

4. Using the point (13 cc, 50 g):

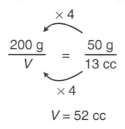

   $$\frac{200\,g}{V} = \frac{50\,g}{13\,cc}$$

   $\times 4$

   $V = 52$ cc

   Using the point (16 cc, 60 g):

   $\times 3.75 \quad \frac{200\,g}{V} = \frac{60\,g}{16\,cc} \quad \times 3.75$

   $V = 53.3$ cc

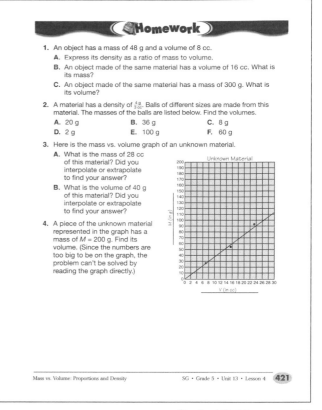

Student Guide - page 421

5. Copy the following table. Then find the density of the objects in the table. Which object has greatest density?

Object	Volume of Object (in cc)	Mass of Object (in g)	Density in g/cc
A	24	11.0	
B	9	11.0	
C	4	5.5	
D	11	5.5	

6. Here is a graph of the mass vs. volume of several materials. Using the graph, tell which of the materials will sink and which will float in water. Explain why.

7. A. Compute the densities of the materials in the graph.
   B. Based on their densities, tell which materials will sink and which will float in water. Explain why.

Student Guide - page 422

Student Guide (p. 422)

5. Object C has the greatest density.

Object	Volume of Object (in cc)	Mass of Object (in g)	Density
A	24	11.0	0.46 g/1 cc
B	9	11.0	1.22 g/1 cc
C	4	5.5	1.38 g/1 cc
D	11	5.5	0.5 g/1 cc

6. The M vs. V line for water would fall between the lines for material B and C, as shown in this graph.

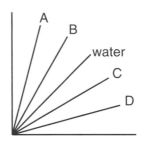

The lines above the line for water (materials A and B) will sink; materials C and D will float. Alternatively, students can use the graph to find $\frac{M}{V}$ ratios for the four materials. Materials A and B have a $\frac{M}{V}$ ratio greater than 1. The ratio of $\frac{M}{V}$ for materials C and D is less than 1. Thus, materials A and B sink and materials C and D float.

7. A. Density of Material A $= \frac{7\,\text{g}}{3\,\text{cc}} = 2.33$ g/cc

   Density of Material B $= \frac{4\,\text{g}}{3\,\text{cc}} = 1.33$ g/cc

   Density of Material C $= \frac{2\,\text{g}}{3\,\text{cc}} = 0.67$ g/cc

   Density of Material D $= \frac{1\,\text{g}}{4\,\text{cc}} = 0.25$ g/cc

B. Since the densities of Materials A and B are greater than 1, these materials will sink in water. Since the densities of Materials C and D are less than 1, these materials will float in water.

Discovery Assignment Book (p. 203)

Home Practice*

Part 4. Measuring the Density of Rocks

1.

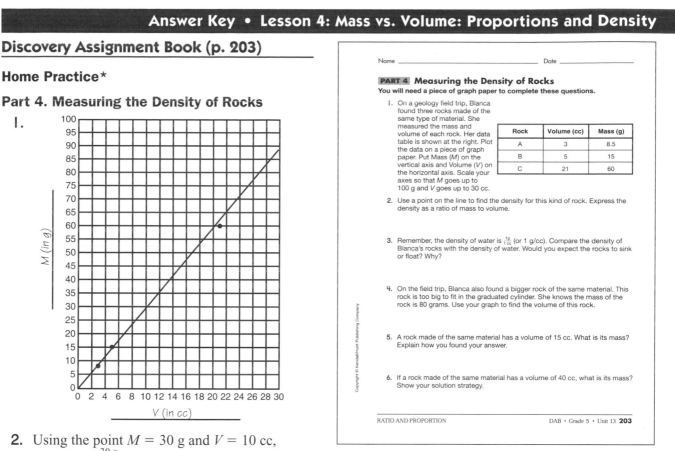

2. Using the point $M = 30$ g and $V = 10$ cc,
   Density $= \frac{30\,g}{10\,cc} = 3$ g/cc

3. Since the density of the rock is greater than 1, the rocks will sink in water.

4. About 27 cc

5. 45 g. Solution strategies will vary. $\frac{3\,g}{1\,cc} = \frac{M}{15\,cc}$;
   $M = 3$ g $\times 15 = 45$ g

6. 120 g. Solution strategies will vary. $\frac{3\,g}{1\,cc} = \frac{M}{40\,cc}$;
   $M = 3$ g $\times 40 = 120$ g

Name _____ Date _____

PART 4 **Measuring the Density of Rocks**
You will need a piece of graph paper to complete these questions.

1. On a geology field trip, Blanca found three rocks made of the same type of material. She measured the mass and volume of each rock. Her data table is shown at the right. Plot the data on a piece of graph paper. Put Mass (*M*) on the vertical axis and Volume (*V*) on the horizontal axis. Scale your axes so that *M* goes up to 100 g and *V* goes up to 30 cc.

Rock	Volume (cc)	Mass (g)
A	3	8.5
B	5	15
C	21	60

2. Use a point on the line to find the density for this kind of rock. Express the density as a ratio of mass to volume.

3. Remember, the density of water is $\frac{1\,g}{1\,cc}$ (or 1 g/cc). Compare the density of Blanca's rocks with the density of water. Would you expect the rocks to sink or float? Why?

4. On the field trip, Blanca also found a bigger rock of the same material. This rock is too big to fit in the graduated cylinder. She knows the mass of the rock is 80 grams. Use your graph to find the volume of this rock.

5. A rock made of the same material has a volume of 15 cc. What is its mass? Explain how you found your answer.

6. If a rock made of the same material has a volume of 40 cc, what is its mass? Show your solution strategy.

RATIO AND PROPORTION   DAB • Grade 5 • Unit 13 **203**

Discovery Assignment Book - page 203

---

*Answers for all the Home Practice in the *Discovery Assignment Book* are at the end of the unit.

Lesson 5

Problems of Scale

Lesson Overview

Students solve a variety of word problems involving proportions. They take a quiz on concepts learned in the unit.

Key Content

- Communicating solutions orally and in writing.
- Choosing appropriate methods and tools to calculate (calculators, paper and pencil, or mental math).
- Using ratios and proportions to solve problems.

Math Facts

DPP item S provides practice with the division facts.

Homework

Assign some or all of the questions for homework.

Assessment

Use the *Paint Quiz* as an assessment.

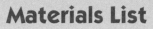

Materials List

Supplies and Copies

Student	Teacher
Supplies for Each Student • calculator • ruler	**Supplies**
Copies • 1 copy of *Paint Quiz* per student (*Unit Resource Guide* Pages 102–103)	**Copies/Transparencies**

All blackline masters including assessment, transparency, and DPP masters are also on the Teacher Resource CD.

Student Books
Problems of Scale (*Student Guide* Page 423)

Daily Practice and Problems and Home Practice
DPP items S–T (*Unit Resource Guide* Pages 22–23)

Note: Classrooms whose pacing differs significantly from the suggested pacing of the units should use the Math Facts Calendar in Section 4 of the *Facts Resource Guide* to ensure students receive the complete math facts program.

Daily Practice and Problems

Suggestions for using the DPPs are below.

S. Bit: Division Fact Practice

$\boxed{\begin{array}{c} 5 \\ \times\ 7 \end{array}}$

(URG p. 22)

A. $16 \div 8 =$ B. $35 \div 7 =$
C. $49 \div 7 =$ D. $40 \div 10 =$
E. $15 \div 5 =$ F. $16 \div 4 =$
G. $50 \div 5 =$ H. $18 \div 2 =$
I. $70 \div 7 =$ J. $20 \div 10 =$
K. $81 \div 9 =$ L. $64 \div 8 =$
M. $6 \div 2 =$ N. $30 \div 5 =$
O. $100 \div 10 =$

T. Challenge: Giant Problems

[N]

(URG p. 23)

1. Lee Yah is telling a story to her little sister. The story is about a giant and a fifth grader. In the story, bodies of the giant and the fifth grader are proportional. The fifth grader is 140 cm tall and her hand is 12 cm long. If the giant's hand is 36 cm long, how tall is the giant?

2. The giant has three sisters. The first sister is $\frac{5}{6}$ as tall as the giant. The second sister is $\frac{5}{7}$ as tall as the giant. The third sister is $\frac{6}{7}$ as tall as the giant.
   A. Which sister is the tallest?
   B. Calculate the heights of the three sisters.

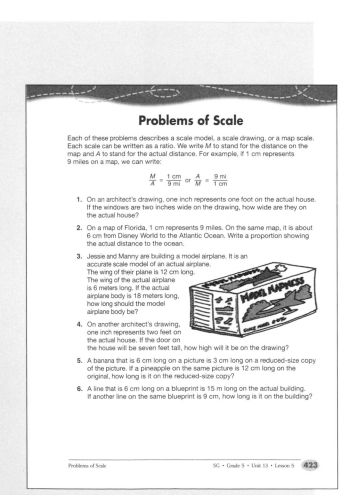

Problems of Scale

Each of these problems describes a scale model, a scale drawing, or a map scale. Each scale can be written as a ratio. We write M to stand for the distance on the map and A to stand for the actual distance. For example, if 1 cm represents 9 miles on a map, we can write:

$$\frac{M}{A} = \frac{1\ cm}{9\ mi} \quad \text{or} \quad \frac{A}{M} = \frac{9\ mi}{1\ cm}$$

1. On an architect's drawing, one inch represents one foot on the actual house. If the windows are two inches wide on the drawing, how wide are they on the actual house?

2. On a map of Florida, 1 cm represents 9 miles. On the same map, it is about 6 cm from Disney World to the Atlantic Ocean. Write a proportion showing the actual distance to the ocean.

3. Jessie and Manny are building a model airplane. It is an accurate scale model of an actual airplane. The wing of their plane is 12 cm long. The wing of the actual airplane is 6 meters long. If the actual airplane body is 18 meters long, how long should the model airplane body be?

4. On another architect's drawing, one inch represents two feet on the actual house. If the door on the house will be seven feet tall, how high will it be on the drawing?

5. A banana that is 6 cm long on a picture is 3 cm long on a reduced-size copy of the picture. If a pineapple on the same picture is 12 cm long on the original, how long is it on the reduced-size copy?

6. A line that is 6 cm long on a blueprint is 15 m long on the actual building. If another line on the same blueprint is 9 cm, how long is it on the building?

Problems of Scale   SG • Grade 5 • Unit 13 • Lesson 5   **423**

Student Guide - page 423 (Answers on p. 104)

Teaching the Activity

This problem set can serve many purposes. It presents opportunities to choose appropriate methods to solve problems. Estimation, paper-and-pencil methods, and calculators are appropriate. It can also supplement homework for the unit.

Once students complete the *Problems of Scale* Activity Page in the *Student Guide,* give them the *Paint Quiz* as an assessment.

Math Facts

DPP item S provides practice with the division facts.

Homework and Practice

- Assign some or all of the questions for homework.
- Assign DPP Challenge T to practice working with proportions.

Assessment

Use the *Paint Quiz* as an assessment.

At a Glance

Math Facts and Daily Practice and Problems

DPP item S provides practice with the division facts. Challenge T develops number sense as students set up proportions to solve problems.

Teaching the Activity

Students complete *Questions 1–6* on the *Problems of Scale* Activity Page in the *Student Guide*.

Homework

Assign some or all of the questions for homework.

Assessment

Use the *Paint Quiz* as an assessment.

Answer Key is on pages 104–105.

Notes:

Paint Quiz

Solve the following problems using ratios and proportions. Show your work.

1. Jessie and Roberto mix red and blue paint to make a purple color they like. To make it, they use a ratio of 2 drops of red to 3 drops of blue. The students want to mix a larger batch so that they can use it to paint.

   A. Write the ratio of red paint to blue paint as a fraction.

   B. Write the ratio of red paint to blue paint using a colon.

2. **A.** If Jessie and Roberto use 4 drops of red, how many drops of blue will they need?

   B. If they use 12 drops of red, how many drops of blue will they need?

   C. If they use 3 cups of blue, how many cups of red will they need?

   D. If they use 1 cup of red, how many cups of blue will they need?

   E. Give three other combinations of red and blue that will give the same purple color they began with.

   F. What is a combination of amounts of red and blue that will not give the same purple color?

3. Jessica's father works in a paint store. He mixes the colors that people select to paint their walls. For a certain shade of blue, he mixes a ratio of 5 parts ultramarine blue to 2 parts lampblack.

   A. Fill in a data table like this to show how much he needs of each color. Find two pairs of numbers that will work for the bottom two rows of the data table.

Number of cc of Blue Paint	Number of cc of Black Paint
5	2
10	4
15	
40	
	30
100	

   B. Write a proportion using ratios in your table.

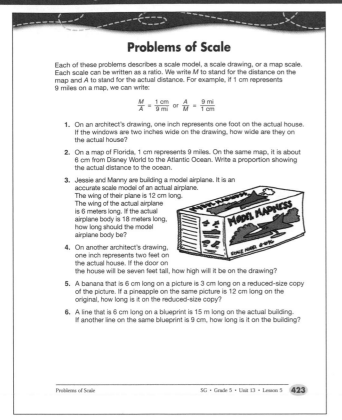

Student Guide - page 423

Student Guide (p. 423)

Problems of Scale

1. $\frac{M}{A} = \frac{1\text{ in}}{1\text{ ft}} = \frac{2\text{ in}}{?\text{ ft}}$; ? = 2 ft

2. $\frac{M}{A} = \frac{1\text{ cm}}{9\text{ mi}} = \frac{6\text{ cm}}{?\text{ mi}}$; ? = 54 mi

3. $\frac{\text{model}}{\text{plane}} = \frac{12\text{ cm}}{6\text{ meters}} = \frac{?\text{ cm}}{18\text{ m}}$; ? = 36 cm

4. $\frac{M}{A} = \frac{1\text{ in}}{2\text{ ft}} = \frac{?\text{ in}}{7\text{ ft}}$; ? = 3.5 in

5. $\frac{\text{original picture}}{\text{reduced size}} = \frac{6\text{ cm}}{3\text{ cm}} = \frac{12\text{ cm}}{?\text{ cm}}$; ? = 6 cm

6. $\frac{M}{A} = \frac{6\text{ cm}}{15\text{ m}} = \frac{9\text{ cm}}{?\text{ m}}$; ? = 22.5 m

Unit Resource Guide (p. 102)

Paint Quiz

1. A. $\frac{2\text{ drops red}}{3\text{ drops blue}}$

   B. 2 drops of red : 3 drops of blue

2. A. 6 drops blue

   B. 18 drops blue

   C. 2 cups red

   D. $1\frac{1}{2}$ cups blue

   E. Answers may vary. Possible solutions include: 6 drops of red and 9 drops of blue; 10 cups of red and 15 cups of blue; 20 drops of red and 30 drops of blue.

   F. Answers may vary. Possible solutions include: 3 drops of red and 4 drops of blue, or 5 drops of red and 6 drops of blue, or 1 cup of red and 3 cups of blue.

Unit Resource Guide - page 102

Unit Resource Guide (p. 103)

3. A.

Number of cc of Blue	Number of cc of Black
5	2
10	4
15	6
40	16
75	30
100	40
110	44
150	60

←— Answers will vary.

B. Answers will vary. One example is:

$$\frac{5 \text{ cc blue}}{2 \text{ cc black}} = \frac{15 \text{ cc blue}}{6 \text{ cc black}}$$

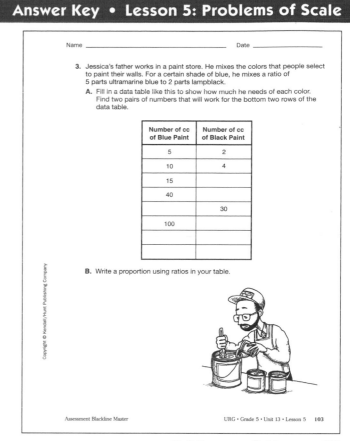

Name _____ Date _____

3. Jessica's father works in a paint store. He mixes the colors that people select to paint their walls. For a certain shade of blue, he mixes a ratio of 5 parts ultramarine blue to 2 parts lampblack.

   A. Fill in a data table like this to show how much he needs of each color. Find two pairs of numbers that will work for the bottom two rows of the data table.

Number of cc of Blue Paint	Number of cc of Black Paint
5	2
10	4
15	
40	
	30
100	

   B. Write a proportion using ratios in your table.

Assessment Blackline Master URG • Grade 5 • Unit 13 • Lesson 5   103

Unit Resource Guide - page 103

Discovery Assignment Book - page 201

Discovery Assignment Book (p. 201)

Part 1. Division Practice

A. 5	B. 2
C. 2	D. 3
E. 10	F. 5
G. 8	H. 6
I. 3	J. 2
K. 5	L. 2
M. 10	N. 7
O. 9	

Part 2. Fractions, Decimals, and Percents

1. A. $16; \frac{4}{5} = \frac{16}{20}$

   B. $40; \frac{9}{10} = \frac{36}{40}$

   C. $7; \frac{4}{7} = \frac{28}{49}$

   D. $1; \frac{1}{8} = \frac{4}{32}$

   E. $30; \frac{5}{6} = \frac{30}{36}$

   F. $80; \frac{3}{4} = \frac{60}{80}$

Discovery Assignment Book - page 202

Discovery Assignment Book (p. 202)

2. A. $\frac{1}{6} < 30\%$

   B. $65\% > \frac{5}{8}$

   C. $\frac{4}{9} < 46\%$

   D. $0.66 < \frac{2}{3}$

   E. $0.43 > \frac{3}{7}$

   F. $\frac{6}{15} = 40\%$

Part 3. Computation Practice

A. 5394	B. 119.6
C. 378 R2	D. 126 R4
E. $8\frac{1}{30}$	F. $2\frac{7}{12}$
G. 24	H. $\frac{1}{2}$
I. 315.45	J. 1071.33
K. 57.64	L. 212.05

Discovery Assignment Book (pp. 203–204)

Part 4. Measuring the Density of Rocks

1.

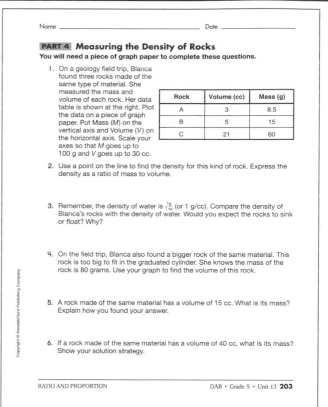

2. Using the point $M = 30$ g and $V = 10$ cc,
Density $= \frac{30\ g}{10\ cc} = 3$ g/cc

3. Since the density of the rock is greater than 1, the rocks will sink in water.

4. About 27 cc

5. 45 g. Solution strategies will vary. $\frac{3\ g}{1\ cc} = \frac{M}{15\ cc}$;
$M = 3$ g $\times 15 = 45$ g

6. 120 g. Solution strategies will vary. $\frac{3\ g}{1\ cc} = \frac{M}{40\ cc}$;
$M = 3$ g $\times 40 = 120$ g

Part 5. In Proportion

1. A. $\frac{14\ chips}{2\ cookies}$ or $\frac{7\ chips}{1\ cookie}$

B. $\frac{35\ chips}{5\ cookies}$ or $\frac{7\ chips}{1\ cookie}$

C. They both have the same ratio, since $\frac{14}{2}$ and $\frac{35}{5}$ both reduce to 7 chips per cookie.

2. A. $3.87

B. $4.30; $0.43

3. A. $6.00

B. $\frac{5}{\$2.00} = \frac{15}{C}$; $C = \$6.00$

Since 15 is 5 $\times$ 3, the price for 15 candy bars is $2.00 $\times$ 3 = $6.00.

4. 6 squirts of red

Name _____ Date _____

PART 4 **Measuring the Density of Rocks**
You will need a piece of graph paper to complete these questions.

1. On a geology field trip, Blanca found three rocks made of the same type of material. She measured the mass and volume of each rock. Her data table is shown at the right. Plot the data on a piece of graph paper. Put Mass (*M*) on the vertical axis and Volume (*V*) on the horizontal axis. Scale your axes so that *M* goes up to 100 g and *V* goes up to 30 cc.

Rock	Volume (cc)	Mass (g)
A	3	8.5
B	5	15
C	21	60

2. Use a point on the line to find the density for this kind of rock. Express the density as a ratio of mass to volume.

3. Remember, the density of water is $\frac{1\ g}{1\ cc}$ (or 1 g/cc). Compare the density of Blanca's rocks with the density of water. Would you expect the rocks to sink or float? Why?

4. On the field trip, Blanca also found a bigger rock of the same material. This rock is too big to fit in the graduated cylinder. She knows the mass of the rock is 80 grams. Use your graph to find the volume of this rock.

5. A rock made of the same material has a volume of 15 cc. What is its mass? Explain how you found your answer.

6. If a rock made of the same material has a volume of 40 cc, what is its mass? Show your solution strategy.

RATIO AND PROPORTION   DAB • Grade 5 • Unit 13 **203**

Discovery Assignment Book - page 203

Name _____ Date _____

PART 5 **In Proportion**
Solve the following problems using pencil and paper or a calculator.

1. David and Felicia both brought chocolate chip cookies for dessert with their lunches.
   A. David counts 14 chips in his two cookies. What is the ratio of chips to cookies in David's lunch?

   B. Felicia counts 35 chips in her 5 cookies. What is the ratio of chips to cookies in Felicia's lunch?

   C. Who has the higher ratio of chocolate chips to cookies? Explain.

2. Notebooks are on sale for 3 for $1.29. Alexis's mother decides to stock up on them.
   A. If she buys nine notebooks, how much will she spend on notebooks?

   B. If she buys ten notebooks, how much will she spend? What does one notebook cost?

3. Candy bars come in packages of 5 for $2.00.
   A. What is the price for 15 candy bars?

   B. Give two different strategies you can use to solve the problem.

4. Arti is mixing some orange paint for the class mural. She mixes 3 squirts of yellow to 2 squirts of red and gets a beautiful orange color. Shannon put 9 squirts of yellow in her bowl. If she wants to get the same orange color as Arti, how many squirts of red should she use?

204 DAB • Grade 5 • Unit 13   RATIO AND PROPORTION

Discovery Assignment Book - page 204

Glossary

This glossary provides definitions of key vocabulary terms in the Grade 5 lessons. Locations of key vocabulary terms in the curriculum are included with each definition. Components Key: URG = *Unit Resource Guide* and SG = *Student Guide*.

A

Acute Angle (URG Unit 6; SG Unit 6)
An angle that measures less than 90°.

Acute Triangle (URG Unit 6 & Unit 15; SG Unit 6 & Unit 15)
A triangle that has only acute angles.

All-Partials Multiplication Method (URG Unit 2)
A paper-and-pencil method for solving multiplication problems. Each partial product is recorded on a separate line. (*See also* partial product.)

$$\begin{array}{r} 186 \\ \times\ 3 \\ \hline 18 \\ 240 \\ 300 \\ \hline 558 \end{array}$$

Altitude of a Triangle (URG Unit 15; SG Unit 15)
A line segment from a vertex of a triangle perpendicular to the opposite side or to the line extending the opposite side; also, the length of this line. The altitude is also called the height of the triangle.

Angle (URG Unit 6; SG Unit 6)
The amount of turning or the amount of opening between two rays that have the same endpoint.

Arc (URG Unit 14; SG Unit 14)
Part of a circle between two points. (*See also* circle.)

Area (URG Unit 4 & Unit 15; SG Unit 4 & Unit 15)
A measurement of size. The area of a shape is the amount of space it covers, measured in square units.

Average (URG Unit 1 & Unit 4; SG Unit 1 & Unit 4)
A number that can be used to represent a typical value in a set of data. (*See also* mean, median, and mode.)

Axes (URG Unit 10; SG Unit 10)
Reference lines on a graph. In the Cartesian coordinate system, the axes are two perpendicular lines that meet at the origin. The singular of axes is axis.

B

Base of a Triangle (URG Unit 15; SG Unit 15)
One of the sides of a triangle; also, the length of the side. A perpendicular line drawn from the vertex opposite the base is called the height or altitude of the triangle.

Base of an Exponent (URG Unit 2; SG Unit 2)
When exponents are used, the number being multiplied. In $3^4 = 3 \times 3 \times 3 \times 3 = 81$, the 3 is the base and the 4 is the exponent. The 3 is multiplied by itself 4 times.

Base-Ten Pieces (URG Unit 2; SG Unit 2)
A set of manipulatives used to model our number system as shown in the figure below. Note that a skinny is made of 10 bits, a flat is made of 100 bits, and a pack is made of 1000 bits.

Base-Ten Shorthand (URG Unit 2)
A graphical representation of the base-ten pieces as shown below.

Nickname	Picture	Shorthand
bit	▱	•
skinny	▭▭▭▭	/
flat	▦	▱
pack	▦	▱

Benchmarks (SG Unit 7)
Numbers convenient for comparing and ordering numbers, e.g., $0, \frac{1}{2}, 1$ are convenient benchmarks for comparing and ordering fractions.

Best-Fit Line (URG Unit 3; SG Unit 3)
The line that comes closest to the points on a point graph.

Binning Data (URG Unit 8; SG Unit 8)
Placing data from a data set with a large number of values or large range into intervals in order to more easily see patterns in the data.

Bit (URG Unit 2; SG Unit 2)
A cube that measures 1 cm on each edge.
It is the smallest of the base-ten pieces and
is often used to represent 1. (*See also* base-ten pieces.)

C

Cartesian Coordinate System (URG Unit 10; SG Unit 10)
A method of locating points on a flat surface by means of an ordered pair of numbers. This method is named after its originator, René Descartes. (*See also* coordinates.)

Categorical Variable (URG Unit 1; SG Unit 1)
Variables with values that are not numbers. (*See also* variable and value.)

Center of a Circle (URG Unit 14; SG Unit 14)
The point such that every point on a circle is the same distance from it. (*See also* circle.)

Centiwheel (URG Unit 7; SG Unit 7)
A circle divided into 100 equal sections used in exploring fractions, decimals, and percents.

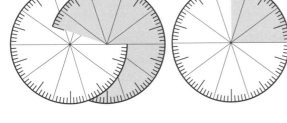

Central Angle (URG Unit 14; SG Unit 14)
An angle whose vertex is at the center of a circle.

Certain Event (URG Unit 7; SG Unit 7)
An event that has a probability of 1 (100%).

Chord (URG Unit 14; SG Unit 14)
A line segment that connects two points on a circle.
(*See also* circle.)

Circle (URG Unit 14; SG Unit 14)
A curve that is made up of all the points that are the same distance from one point, the center.

Circumference (URG Unit 14; SG Unit 14)
The distance around a circle.

Common Denominator (URG Unit 5 & Unit 11; SG Unit 5 & Unit 11)
A denominator that is shared by two or more fractions. A common denominator is a common multiple of the denominators of the fractions. 15 is a common denominator of $\frac{2}{3} (= \frac{10}{15})$ and $\frac{4}{5} (= \frac{12}{15})$ since 15 is divisible by both 3 and 5.

Common Fraction (URG Unit 7; SG Unit 7)
Any fraction that is written with a numerator and denominator that are whole numbers. For example, $\frac{3}{4}$ and $\frac{9}{4}$ are both common fractions. (*See also* decimal fraction.)

Commutative Property of Addition (URG Unit 2)
The order of the addends in an addition problem does not matter, e.g., $7 + 3 = 3 + 7$.

Commutative Property of Multiplication (URG Unit 2)
The order of the factors in a multiplication problem does not matter, e.g., $7 \times 3 = 3 \times 7$. (*See also* turn-around facts.)

Compact Method (URG Unit 2)
Another name for what is considered the traditional multiplication algorithm.

$$\begin{array}{r} \overset{2\ 1}{186} \\ \times\ 3 \\ \hline 558 \end{array}$$

Composite Number (URG Unit 11; SG Unit 11)
A number that has more than two distinct factors. For example, 9 has three factors (1, 3, 9) so it is a composite number.

Concentric Circles (URG Unit 14; SG Unit 14)
Circles that have the same center.

Congruent (URG Unit 6 & Unit 10; SG Unit 6)
Figures that are the same shape and size. Polygons are congruent when corresponding sides have the same length and corresponding angles have the same measure.

Conjecture (URG Unit 11; SG Unit 11)
A statement that has not been proved to be true, nor shown to be false.

Convenient Number (URG Unit 2; SG Unit 2)
A number used in computation that is close enough to give a good estimate, but is also easy to compute with mentally, e.g., 25 and 30 are convenient numbers for 27.

Convex (URG Unit 6)
A shape is convex if for any two points in the shape, the line segment between the points is also inside the shape.

Coordinates (URG Unit 10; SG Unit 10)
An ordered pair of numbers that locates points on a flat surface relative to a pair of coordinate axes. For example, in the ordered pair (4, 5), the first number (coordinate) is the distance from the point to the vertical axis and the second coordinate is the distance from the point to the horizontal axis. (*See also* axes.)

Corresponding Parts (URG Unit 10; SG Unit 10)
Matching parts in two or more figures. In the figure
below, Sides AB and A'B' are corresponding parts.

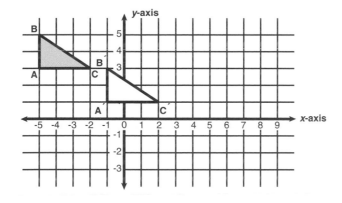

Cryptography (SG Unit 11) The study of secret codes.

Cubic Centimeter (URG Unit 13)
The volume of a cube that is one centimeter long on
each edge.

D

Data (SG Unit 1)
Information collected in an experiment or survey.

Decagon (URG Unit 6; SG Unit 6)
A ten-sided, ten-angled polygon.

Decimal (URG Unit 7; SG Unit 7)
1. A number written using the base ten place value
   system.
2. A number containing a decimal point.

Decimal Fraction (URG Unit 7; SG Unit 7)
A fraction written as a decimal. For example, 0.75 and
0.4 are decimal fractions and $\frac{75}{100}$ and $\frac{4}{10}$ are the equivalent
common fractions.

Degree (URG Unit 6; SG Unit 6)
A degree (°) is a unit of measure for angles. There are
360 degrees in a circle.

Denominator (URG Unit 3; SG Unit 3)
The number below the line in a fraction. The denominator indicates the number of equal parts in which the unit
whole is divided. For example, the 5 is the denominator
in the fraction $\frac{2}{5}$. In this case the unit whole is divided into
five equal parts. (*See also* numerator.)

Density (URG Unit 13; SG Unit 13)
The ratio of an object's mass to its volume.

Diagonal (URG Unit 6)
A line segment that connects nonadjacent corners of
a polygon.

Diameter (URG Unit 14; SG Unit 14)
1. A line segment that connects two points on a circle
   and passes through the center.
2. The length of this line segment.

Digit (SG Unit 2)
Any one of the ten symbols 0, 1, 2, 3, 4, 5, 6, 7, 8, 9.
The number 37 is made up of the digits 3 and 7.

Dividend (URG Unit 4 & Unit 9; SG Unit 4 & Unit 9)
The number that is divided in a division problem,
e.g., 12 is the dividend in $12 \div 3 = 4$.

Divisor (URG Unit 2, Unit 4, & Unit 9; SG Unit 2,
   Unit 4, & Unit 9)
In a division problem, the number by which another
number is divided. In the problem $12 \div 4 = 3$, the 4
is the divisor, the 12 is the dividend, and the 3 is the
quotient.

Dodecagon (URG Unit 6; SG Unit 6)
A twelve-sided, twelve-angled polygon.

E

Endpoint (URG Unit 6; SG Unit 6)
The point at either end of a line segment or the point at
the end of a ray.

Equally Likely (URG Unit 7; SG Unit 7)
When events have the same probability, they are called
equally likely.

Equidistant (URG Unit 14)
At the same distance.

Equilateral Triangle (URG Unit 6, Unit 14, & Unit 15)
A triangle that has all three sides equal in length. An
equilateral triangle also has three equal angles.

Equivalent Fractions (URG Unit 3; SG Unit 3)
Fractions that have the same value, e.g., $\frac{2}{4} = \frac{1}{2}$.

Estimate (URG Unit 2; SG Unit 2)
1. To find *about* how many (as a verb).
2. A number that is *close to* the desired number (as a
   noun).

Expanded Form (SG Unit 2)
A way to write numbers that shows the place value of
each digit, e.g., $4357 = 4000 + 300 + 50 + 7$.

Exponent (URG Unit 2 & Unit 11; SG Unit 2 & Unit 11)
The number of times the base is multiplied by itself.
In $3^4 = 3 \times 3 \times 3 \times 3 = 81$, the 3 is the base and the
4 is the exponent. The 3 is multiplied by itself 4 times.

Extrapolation (URG Unit 13; SG Unit 13)
Using patterns in data to make predictions or to estimate
values that lie beyond the range of values in the set of
data.

F

Fact Families (URG Unit 2; SG Unit 2)
Related math facts, e.g., $3 \times 4 = 12$, $4 \times 3 = 12$,
$12 \div 3 = 4$, $12 \div 4 = 3$.

Factor Tree (URG Unit 11; SG Unit 11)
A diagram that shows the prime factorization of a number.

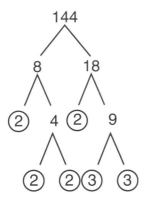

Factors (URG Unit 2 & Unit 11; SG Unit 2 & Unit 11)
1. In a multiplication problem, the numbers that are multiplied together. In the problem $3 \times 4 = 12$, 3 and 4 are the factors.
2. Numbers that divide a number evenly, e.g., 1, 2, 3, 4, 6, and 12 are all the factors of 12.

Fair Game (URG Unit 7; SG Unit 7)
A game in which it is equally likely that any player will win.

Fewest Pieces Rule (URG Unit 2)
Using the least number of base-ten pieces to represent a number. (*See also* base-ten pieces.)

Fixed Variables (URG Unit 4; SG Unit 3 & Unit 4)
Variables in an experiment that are held constant or not changed, in order to find the relationship between the manipulated and responding variables. These variables are often called controlled variables. (*See also* manipulated variable and responding variable.)

Flat (URG Unit 2; SG Unit 2)
A block that measures 1 cm $\times$ 10 cm $\times$ 10 cm. It is one of the base-ten pieces and is often used to represent 100. (*See also* base-ten pieces.)

Flip (URG Unit 10; SG Unit 10)
A motion of the plane in which the plane is reflected over a line so that any point and its image are the same distance from the line.

Forgiving Division Method
(URG Unit 4; SG Unit 4)
A paper-and-pencil method for division in which successive partial quotients are chosen and subtracted from the dividend, until the remainder is less than the divisor. The sum of the partial quotients is the quotient. For example, $644 \div 7$ can be solved as shown at the right.

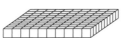

Formula (SG Unit 11 & Unit 14)
A number sentence that gives a general rule. A formula for finding the area of a rectangle is Area = length $\times$ width, or $A = l \times w$.

Fraction (URG Unit 7; SG Unit 7)
A number that can be written as a/b where a and b are whole numbers and b is not zero.

G

Googol (URG Unit 2)
A number that is written as a 1 with 100 zeroes after it (10^{100}).

Googolplex (URG Unit 2)
A number that is written as a 1 with a googol of zeroes after it.

H

Height of a Triangle (URG Unit 15; SG Unit 15)
A line segment from a vertex of a triangle perpendicular to the opposite side or to the line extending the opposite side; also, the length of this line. The height is also called the altitude.

Hexagon (URG Unit 6; SG Unit 6)
A six-sided polygon.

Hypotenuse (URG Unit 15; SG Unit 15)
The longest side of a right triangle.

I

Image (URG Unit 10; SG Unit 10)
The result of a transformation, in particular a slide (translation) or a flip (reflection), in a coordinate plane. The new figure after the slide or flip is the image of the old figure.

Impossible Event (URG Unit 7; SG Unit 7)
An event that has a probability of 0 or 0%.

Improper Fraction (URG Unit 3; SG Unit 3)
A fraction in which the numerator is greater than or equal to the denominator. An improper fraction is greater than or equal to one.

Infinite (URG Unit 2)
Never ending, immeasurably great, unlimited.

Interpolation (URG Unit 13; SG Unit 13)
Making predictions or estimating values that lie between data points in a set of data.

Intersect (URG Unit 14)
To meet or cross.

Isosceles Triangle (URG Unit 6 & Unit 15)
A triangle that has at least two sides of equal length.

J

K

L

Lattice Multiplication
(URG Unit 9; SG Unit 9)
A method for multiplying that
uses a lattice to arrange the
partial products so the digits are
correctly placed in the correct
place value columns. A lattice
for 43 × 96 = 4128 is shown at
the right.

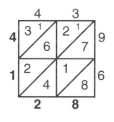

Legs of a Right Triangle (URG Unit 15; SG Unit 15)
The two sides of a right triangle that form the right angle.

Length of a Rectangle (URG Unit 4 & Unit 15;
SG Unit 4 & Unit 15)
The distance along one side of a rectangle.

Line
A set of points that form a straight path extending infi-
nitely in two directions.

Line of Reflection (URG Unit 10)
A line that acts as a mirror so that after a shape is flipped
over the line, corresponding points are at the same distance (equidistant) from the line.

Line Segment (URG Unit 14)
A part of a line between and including two points, called
the endpoints.

Liter (URG Unit 13)
Metric unit used to measure volume. A liter is a little
more than a quart.

Lowest Terms (SG Unit 11)
A fraction is in lowest terms if the numerator and
denominator have no common factor greater than 1.

M

Manipulated Variable (URG Unit 4; SG Unit 4)
In an experiment, the variable with values known at the
beginning of the experiment. The experimenter often
chooses these values before data is collected. The manipulated variable is often called the independent variable.

Mass (URG Unit 13)
The amount of matter in an object.

Mean (URG Unit 1 & Unit 4; SG Unit 1 & Unit 4)
An average of a set of numbers that is found by adding
the values of the data and dividing by the number of
values.

Measurement Division (URG Unit 4)
Division as equal grouping. The total number of objects
and the number of objects in each group are known. The
number of groups is the unknown. For example, tulip
bulbs come in packages of 8. If 216 bulbs are sold, how
many packages are sold?

Median (URG Unit 1; SG Unit 1)
For a set with an odd number of data arranged in order,
it is the middle number. For an even number of data
arranged in order, it is the mean of the two middle
numbers.

Meniscus (URG Unit 13)
The curved surface formed when a liquid creeps up the
side of a container (for example, a graduated cylinder).

Milliliter (ml) (URG Unit 13)
A measure of capacity in the metric system that is the
volume of a cube that is one centimeter long on each
side.

Mixed Number (URG Unit 3; SG Unit 3)
A number that is written as a whole number followed by
a fraction. It is equal to the sum of the whole number and
the fraction.

Mode (URG Unit 1; SG Unit 1)
The most common value in a data set.

Mr. Origin (URG Unit 10; SG Unit 10)
A plastic figure used to represent the origin of a coordinate system and to indicate the directions of the x- and
y- axes. (and possibly the z-axis).

N

N-gon (URG Unit 6; SG Unit 6)
A polygon with N sides.

Negative Number (URG Unit 10; SG Unit 10)
A number less than zero; a number to the left of zero on a
horizontal number line.

Nonagon (URG Unit 6; SG Unit 6)
A nine-sided polygon.

Numerator (URG Unit 3; SG Unit 3)
The number written above the line in a fraction. For
example, the 2 is the numerator in the fraction $\frac{2}{5}$. In this
case, we are interested in two of the five parts. (*See also*
denominator.)

Numerical Expression (URG Unit 4; SG Unit 4)
A combination of numbers and operations, e.g.,
$5 + 8 \div 4$.

Numerical Variable (URG Unit 1; SG Unit 1)
Variables with values that are numbers. (*See also* variable
and value.)

O

Obtuse Angle (URG Unit 6; SG Unit 6)
An angle that measures more than 90°.

Obtuse Triangle (URG Unit 6 & Unit 15; SG Unit 6 & Unit 15)
A triangle that has an obtuse angle.

Octagon (URG Unit 6; SG Unit 6)
An eight-sided polygon.

Ordered Pair (URG Unit 10; SG Unit 10)
A pair of numbers that gives the coordinates of a point on a grid in relation to the origin. The horizontal coordinate is given first; the vertical coordinate is given second. For example, the ordered pair (5, 3) gives the coordinates of the point that is 5 units to the right of the origin and 3 units up.

Origin (URG Unit 10; SG Unit 10)
The point at which the *x*- and *y*-axes intersect on a coordinate plane. The origin is described by the ordered pair (0, 0) and serves as a reference point so that all the points on the plane can be located by ordered pairs.

P

Pack (URG Unit 2; SG Unit 2)
A cube that measures 10 cm on each edge. It is one of the base-ten pieces and is often used to represent 1000. (*See also* base-ten pieces.)

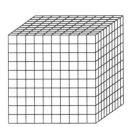

Parallel Lines
(URG Unit 6 & Unit 10)
Lines that are in the same direction. In the plane, parallel lines are lines that do not intersect.

Parallelogram (URG Unit 6)
A quadrilateral with two pairs of parallel sides.

Partial Product (URG Unit 2)
One portion of the multiplication process in the all-partials multiplication method, e.g., in the problem 3 × 186 there are three partial products: 3 × 6 = 18, 3 × 80 = 240, and 3 × 100 = 300. (*See also* all-partials multiplication method.)

Partitive Division (URG Unit 4)
Division as equal sharing. The total number of objects and the number of groups are known. The number of objects in each group is the unknown. For example, Frank has 144 marbles that he divides equally into 6 groups. How many marbles are in each group?

Pentagon (URG Unit 6; SG Unit 6)
A five-sided polygon.

Percent (URG Unit 7; SG Unit 7)
Per hundred or out of 100. A special ratio that compares a number to 100. For example, 20% (twenty percent) of the jelly beans are yellow means that out of every 100 jelly beans, 20 are yellow.

Perimeter (URG Unit 15; SG Unit 15)
The distance around a two-dimensional shape.

Period (SG Unit 2)
A group of three places in a large number, starting on the right, often separated by commas as shown at the right.

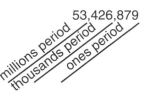

Perpendicular Lines (URG Unit 14 & Unit 15; SG Unit 14)
Lines that meet at right angles.

Pi (π) (URG Unit 14; SG Unit 14)
The ratio of the circumference to diameter of a circle. π = 3.14159265358979. . . . It is a nonterminating, nonrepeating decimal.

Place (SG Unit 2)
The position of a digit in a number.

Place Value (URG Unit 2; SG Unit 2)
The value of a digit in a number. For example, the 5 is in the hundreds place in 4573, so it stands for 500.

Polygon (URG Unit 6; SG Unit 6)
A two-dimensional connected figure made of line segments in which each endpoint of every side meets with an endpoint of exactly one other side.

Population (URG Unit 1 Unit 1)
A collection of persons or things whose properties will be analyzed in a survey or experiment.

Portfolio (URG Unit 2; SG Unit 2)
A collection of student work that show how a student's skills, attitudes, and knowledge change over time.

Positive Number (URG Unit 10; SG Unit 10)
A number greater than zero; a number to the right of zero on a horizontal number line.

Power (URG Unit 2; SG Unit 2)
An exponent. Read 10^4 as, "ten to the fourth power" or "ten to the fourth." We say 10,000 or 10^4 is the fourth power of ten.

Prime Factorization (URG Unit 11; SG Unit 11)
Writing a number as a product of primes. The prime factorization of 100 is 2 × 2 × 5 × 5.

Prime Number (URG Unit 11; SG Unit 11)
A number that has exactly two factors: itself and 1. For example, 7 has exactly two distinct factors, 1 and 7.

Probability (URG Unit 7; SG Unit 1 & Unit 7)
A number from 0 to 1 (0% to 100%) that describes how likely an event is to happen. The closer that the probability of an event is to one, the more likely the event will happen.

Product (URG Unit 2; SG Unit 2)
The answer to a multiplication problem. In the problem $3 \times 4 = 12$, 12 is the product.

Proper Fraction (URG Unit 3; SG Unit 3)
A fraction in which the numerator is less than the denominator. Proper fractions are less than one.

Proportion (URG Unit 3 & Unit 13; SG Unit 13)
A statement that two ratios are equal.

Protractor (URG Unit 6; SG Unit 6)
A tool for measuring angles.

Q

Quadrants (URG Unit 10; SG Unit 10)
The four sections of a coordinate grid that are separated by the axes.

Quadrilateral (URG Unit 6; SG Unit 6)
A polygon with four sides. (*See also* polygon.)

Quotient (URG Unit 4 & Unit 9; SG Unit 2, Unit 4, & Unit 9)
The answer to a division problem. In the problem $12 \div 3 = 4$, the 4 is the quotient.

R

Radius (URG Unit 14; SG Unit 14)
1. A line segment connecting the center of a circle to any point on the circle.
2. The length of this line segment.

Ratio (URG Unit 3 & Unit 12; SG Unit 3 & Unit 13)
A way to compare two numbers or quantities using division. It is often written as a fraction.

Ray (URG Unit 6; SG Unit 6)
A part of a line with one endpoint that extends indefinitely in one direction.

Rectangle (URG Unit 6; SG Unit 6)
A quadrilateral with four right angles.

Reflection (URG Unit 10)
(*See* flip.)

Regular Polygon (URG Unit 6; SG Unit 6; DAB Unit 6)
A polygon with all sides of equal length and all angles equal.

Remainder (URG Unit 4 & Unit 9; SG Unit 4 & Unit 9)
Something that remains or is left after a division problem. The portion of the dividend that is not evenly divisible by the divisor, e.g., $16 \div 5 = 3$ with 1 as a remainder.

Repeating Decimals (SG Unit 9)
A decimal fraction with one or more digits repeating without end.

Responding Variable (URG Unit 4; SG Unit 4)
The variable whose values result from the experiment. Experimenters find the values of the responding variable by doing the experiment. The responding variable is often called the dependent variable.

Rhombus (URG Unit 6; SG Unit 6)
A quadrilateral with four equal sides.

Right Angle (URG Unit 6; SG Unit 6)
An angle that measures 90°.

Right Triangle (URG Unit 6 & Unit 15; SG Unit 6 & Unit 15)
A triangle that contains a right angle.

Rubric (URG Unit 1)
A scoring guide that can be used to guide or assess student work.

S

Sample (URG Unit 1)
A part or subset of a population.

Scalene Triangle (URG Unit 15)
A triangle that has no sides that are equal in length.

Scientific Notation (URG Unit 2; SG Unit 2)
A way of writing numbers, particularly very large or very small numbers. A number in scientific notation has two factors. The first factor is a number greater than or equal to one and less than ten. The second factor is a power of 10 written with an exponent. For example, 93,000,000 written in scientific notation is 9.3×10^7.

Septagon (URG Unit 6; SG Unit 6)
A seven-sided polygon.

Side-Angle-Side (URG Unit 6 & Unit 14)
A geometric property stating that two triangles having two corresponding sides with the included angle equal are congruent.

Side-Side-Side (URG Unit 6)
A geometric property stating that two triangles having corresponding sides equal are congruent.

Sides of an Angle (URG Unit 6; SG Unit 6)
The sides of an angle are two rays with the same endpoint. (*See also* endpoint and ray.)

Sieve of Eratosthenes (SG Unit 11)
A method for separating prime numbers from nonprime numbers developed by Eratosthenes, an Egyptian librarian, in about 240 BCE.

Similar (URG Unit 6; SG Unit 6)
Similar shapes have the same shape but not necessarily the same size.

Skinny (URG Unit 2; SG Unit 2)
A block that measures 1 cm × 1 cm × 10 cm.
It is one of the base-ten pieces
and is often used to represent 10.
(*See also* base-ten pieces.)

Slide (URG Unit 10; SG Unit 10)
Moving a geometric figure in the plane by moving every point of the figure the same distance in the same direction. Also called translation.

Speed (URG Unit 3 & Unit 5; SG Unit 3 & Unit 5)
The ratio of distance moved to time taken, e.g., 3 miles/1 hour or 3 mph is a speed.

Square (URG Unit 6 & Unit 14; SG Unit 6)
A quadrilateral with four equal sides and four right angles.

Square Centimeter (URG Unit 4; SG Unit 4)
The area of a square that is 1 cm long on each side.

Square Number (URG Unit 11)
A number that is the product of a whole number multiplied by itself. For example, 25 is a square number since $5 \times 5 = 25$. A square number can be represented by a square array with the same number of rows as columns. A square array for 25 has 5 rows of 5 objects in each row or 25 total objects.

Standard Form (SG Unit 2)
The traditional way to write a number, e.g., standard form for three hundred fifty-seven is 357. (*See also* expanded form and word form.)

Standard Units (URG Unit 4)
Internationally or nationally agreed-upon units used in measuring variables, e.g., centimeters and inches are standard units used to measure length and square centimeters and square inches are used to measure area.

Straight Angle (URG Unit 6; SG Unit 6)
An angle that measures 180º.

T

Ten Percent (URG Unit 4; SG Unit 4)
10 out of every hundred or $\frac{1}{10}$.

Tessellation (URG Unit 6 & Unit 10; SG Unit 6)
A pattern made up of one or more repeated shapes that completely covers a surface without any gaps or overlaps.

Translation
(*See* slide.)

Trapezoid (URG Unit 6)
A quadrilateral with exactly one pair of parallel sides.

Triangle (URG Unit 6; SG Unit 6)
A polygon with three sides.

Triangulating (URG Unit 6; SG Unit 6)
Partitioning a polygon into two or more nonoverlapping triangles by drawing diagonals that do not intersect.

Turn-Around Facts (URG Unit 2)
Multiplication facts that have the same factors but in a different order, e.g., $3 \times 4 = 12$ and $4 \times 3 = 12$. (*See also* commutative property of multiplication.)

Twin Primes (URG Unit 11; SG Unit 11)
A pair of prime numbers whose difference is 2. For example, 3 and 5 are twin primes.

U

Unit Ratio (URG Unit 13; SG Unit 13)
A ratio with a denominator of one.

V

Value (URG Unit 1; SG Unit 1)
The possible outcomes of a variable. For example, red, green, and blue are possible values for the variable *color*. Two meters and 1.65 meters are possible values for the variable *length*.

Variable (URG Unit 1; SG Unit 1)
1. An attribute or quantity that changes or varies. (*See also* categorical variable and numerical variable.)
2. A symbol that can stand for a variable.

Variables in Proportion (URG Unit 13; SG Unit 13)
When the ratio of two variables in an experiment is always the same, the variables are in proportion.

Velocity (URG Unit 5; SG Unit 5)
Speed in a given direction. Speed is the ratio of the distance traveled to time taken.

Vertex (URG Unit 6; SG Unit 6)
A common point of two rays or line segments that form an angle.

Volume (URG Unit 13)
The measure of the amount of space occupied by an object.

W

Whole Number
Any of the numbers 0, 1, 2, 3, 4, 5, 6 and so on.

Width of a Rectangle (URG Unit 4 & Unit 15; SG Unit 4 & Unit 15)
The distance along one side of a rectangle is the length and the distance along an adjacent side is the width.

Word Form (SG Unit 2)
A number expressed in words, e.g., the word form for 123 is "one hundred twenty-three." (*See also* expanded form and standard form.)

X

Y

Z